AF779580

Overcoming Anxiety, Depression and Other Mental Health Disorders in Children and Adults:

A New Roadmap for Families and Professionals

Stanley I. Greenspan, M.D.

Published by the Interdisciplinary Council on
Developmental and Learning Disorders (ICDL)
4938 Hampden Lane, Suite 800
Bethesda, Maryland 20814
www.icdl.com

Copyright ©2009 by Stanley I. Greenspan, M.D.
All rights reserved.
ISBN 0-9767758-8-3

Dedication

This book is dedicated to all those who experience anxiety, depression and other common mental health challenges.

Acknowledgements

Thank you to Jane LaRoque, Sue Morrisson and Deirdre Schwiesow for their help in editing this manuscript.

Contents

Introduction

While there is no substitute for professional therapeutic intervention when needed, there is much that non-professionals can do to help others, and themselves, when confronted with mental health challenges. By providing insights into the developmental pathways leading to the most common health challenges and disorders, this book is aimed at all those who wish greater understanding of these issues. Our framework for dealing with these issues is a model of mental health that can be practiced by people living in community with one another. That community can in essence become a security blanket, like the blanket carried by Linus throughout his comic strip life.

This book explains, first of all, the characteristics of the environments, family patterns, relationships, and experiences that can help people overcome or make progress with mental health challenges. It provides a process for families and other communities to create supportive environments where mental health can flourish and where various mental health disorders may be prevented, softened in their intensity, or moved along a path of recovery. In a nutshell, the general features of these environments are that they are regulating, engaging in terms of relationships, and help the individual experience, understand, and communicate the different emotions of life. The supportive environment can help patch a person's tattered security blanket where needed.

Then we look at the specific disorders themselves, and how to tailor the environment to best help individuals with anxiety, depression, and other challenges. We explore the developmental pathways leading to each disorder, based on our best current understanding, because each pathway provides clues for creating environments that help individuals make progress toward overcoming these disorders. This is a much more comprehensive and developmentally-based approach than is typical when treating mental health disorders. Rather than using just psychotherapy or medication, we focus on the important role of the home, school, and other supportive environments in helping individuals prevent and overcome mental health challenges. We all live in communities, but some communities are better defined and supportive than others.

The following chapters describe caregiver-child interaction patterns that can promote healthy development. They also describe relationships between individuals of any age that tend to support mental health. It should be recognized that as human beings we all have strengths and weaknesses and we all vary considerably in our ability to carry out these "ideal patterns." The suggestions presented in this book are intended as a general guide, meant to inspire rather than provoke guilt or blame.

Chapter 1

The Interaction of Biology and Environment: The DIR Model

Underlying the mental health-promoting process described in this book is a model of mental health disorders that is complex, dynamic, and developmental; to use a technical term, it is a developmental bio-psychosocial model. This means that we consider the environmental factors that contribute to mental illness, the genetic component typically associated with mental illnesses such as depression and bipolar disorder, and also the genetic predispositions toward traits such as reactivity that may be exacerbated by the environment. In fact, it's been shown that almost all mental health disorders result from the complex interplay of the biological component, the experiential or relationship component, and the individual way in which biology expresses itself, in terms of sensory processing and the way in which the person plans and takes actions.

The Developmental, Individual-difference, Relationship-based (DIR) Model, used to frame the processes and techniques in this book, looks at how the factors listed above interact. The "Developmental" aspect refers to the capacities we want to promote, such as engagement, expression of feelings, and gray-area and reflective thinking. The "Individual-difference" aspect reflects the biology of the individual, not in terms of the genetic predisposition for a mental health problem such as bipolar disorder or schizophrenia, but how an individual's biology affects his nervous system at each age or stage of development—as a two-year-old, as a four-year-old, as a 10-year-old, and so forth. For example, we have observed that individuals prone to anxiety or to depression are more sensory-reactive; they are more sensitive to touch and/or sound and/or lights than are other children or other adults. Individuals prone to risk-taking and impulsivity tend to crave sensation and be under-reactive to it; they take risks to get more movement or more feeling tone in their bodies. And individuals prone to disorders such as ADHD often have problems with what we call motor planning and sequencing; they can't sequence many actions in a row and they might have a hard time sequencing their thoughts.

Each disorder has its own profile of individual differences in nervous system functioning, based on how genetics or biology (such as the uterine life) affects the nervous system. Our current understanding is that someone can have a general biological tendency toward a mental illness, which can then be set in motion by certain processes, namely, environmental conditions and relationships.

And that takes us into the "Relationship" aspect of the DIR model. The relationships that promote mental health are tailored to the biological differences of the person with mental health challenges. They are soothing for the hyper-reactive person, containing for the impulsive person, and so forth, which helps the individual progress to higher and higher developmental levels. So, for example, a child may be hyper-reactive to sound (a cat's meow sounds like a lion's roar to him). When his environment is also hyper-reactive, that is, the people around him react to his anxiety with more anxiety, then we get an anxious, fearful child. On the other hand, if the environment is balancing or counter-regulating by being extra soothing, and yet fosters assertiveness, that potentially anxious child may get more comfortable with being assertive and may also learn to calm himself down and eventually become less anxious. He may still be a little prone to anxiety, but it won't be nearly as intense or severe. So, there's a biological potential, but the environment determines which way it goes. This is not to put the blame on the caregivers, who themselves may be prone to anxiety, but knowledge can go a long way with flexible adults who are trying to help children. The same is true between adults as well. A person who knows what a good counterbalancing response is can help his or her anxious spouse calm down.

Therefore, within our developmental bio-psychosocial model, we don't look for a one-to-one relationship between a particular gene and a disorder; we haven't found this connection. Instead, there are usually multiple genes and complex developmental pathways involved. We can identify key points—at two months of life, at four months of life, at 12 months of life, at 24 months of life, and so forth—on the developmental pathways leading to disorders. Disorders don't appear out of the blue; they have a developmental progression. They occur in steps. The more of these steps we can identify, and the more we can discover which capacities develop at each step and how the biological differences are being expressed at each step, the more clear we can be about what sort of relationships will either promote health or contribute to the expression of a disorder at that step. This model enables us to create environments that promote mental health and help individuals overcome each type of disorder.

Defining Mental Health

Within this model, we define mental health not simply as being happy or outgoing or successful career-wise; seemingly happy people can be depressed underneath, outgoing people can be insecure, and superficial traits don't necessarily convey the stability and depth and true mental health of the person. Instead, the way we define mental health is to describe the mentally healthy person as someone who is capable of experiencing the full range of life's emotions at each developmental phase of life, in a broad, comprehensive, stable, and deep manner.

Specifically, the DIR model describes a series of developmental stages: the ability to take interest in the world and be calm and regulated, to engage with depth and intimacy, to exchange and read emotional gestures, to interact with emotional gestures to solve problems with others, to create ideas, to build logical bridges between ideas, to think in a multi-causal framework, to see shades of gray in one's ideas and relationships and feelings, and, finally, to think reflectively—to operate in two frames of reference at the same time. Then, this reflective thinking ability broadens throughout adulthood to embrace more experiences—separation from parents, having a career, rearing children, and so forth—while at the same time maintaining through each of these experiences the ability to incorporate all the emotions of life, from sadness to anger to jealousy to contentment to glorious joy. For example, there's a difference between a person who thinks creatively in terms of aggression, but not in terms of happiness and intimacy, or vice-versa, and someone who can think creatively about all the feelings of life. (For more in-depth information about these stages, see *The Growth of the Mind*, *The First Idea*, and our book on the *Functional and Emotional Assessment Scale*.)

Mental health involves the ability to master each of these basic developmental stages at the appropriate age, or at least to be on a path towards mastery at a slightly later age. Another component of mental health is to feel the full range of feelings with true depth. Some feelings, such as true love and compassion, require a sustaining intimate relationship; a number of superficial social relationships don't provide the same depth or intimacy. Also, the feelings have to be experienced in a stable way at each stage, so that stress doesn't derail us and cause us to lose the abilities of the stage. For example, there's a real difference between a person who can be a gray-area thinker and see the shades of subtlety and nuance in relationships consistently, and one who loses that ability under the pressure of strong feelings (who may have the ability when it comes to casual friendships but not in an intimate relationship, for example), and then reverts to polarized emotional states where everything is perceived as all good or all bad.

So our definition of mental health, then, is the capacity for mastering the age-appropriate developmental stages (or to be on the road toward mastering each stage), with a broad range of age-expected feelings and relationship patterns and activities, and to master these stages to their full depth and breadth, in a stable manner where expectable stresses and strains don't cause the loss of the developmental capacity or a narrowing of the range of feelings the person is capable of experiencing. Thus, mental health is not simply the absence of symptoms; it's the way in which we fully engage in life's expectable dimensions, including, at times, feeling sadness or anger, etc., when circumstances present themselves that naturally lead to those kinds of feelings.

Defining Mental Health Disorders

How, then, do we define mental health disorders? Rather than define them according to their symptoms, a far better way to think about them is in terms of the degree to which the individual deviates from, hasn't fully mastered, or has lost the capacities that we defined above as reflecting mental health. Before we look at specific patterns, we should ask the following questions.

First, does the individual have a deficit in his mastery of any of the age-expected fundamental capacities for regulation, engagement, creative use of ideas and feelings, or reflection? Is she an adult who is unable to do the kind of reflective thinking that is normally mastered in early adolescence, or who is superficial in her patterns of engagement, or who doesn't engage at all, or who can't read and respond to other people's emotional signals at an intuitive, visceral level? If she hasn't mastered a particular stage, then there is a deficit in a fundamental capacity.

If there's no deficit in the fundamental capacity, we then ask the second question. Is there a constriction or a limitation in the range of feelings that can become incorporated into any one of these stages? For example, does the person have mastery of the stage when it comes to anger, but not for intimacy and happiness? If he has a wide range of feelings, then we go to the third question. How deeply can the person experience this wide range of feelings? Are the feelings superficial or deeply felt? If they have depth, then we go to the fourth question. How stable is the mastery of the particular stage? How well does the person do under stress? If he loses his abilities, does he bounce back quickly, or not for a long period of time?

Within this framework, we can characterize mental health disorders according to whether the person has a deficit in the fundamental capacities, a constriction in the range of feelings, a constriction in the depth of feelings, or an instability in the degree to which he can hold on to a particular stage, range of feelings, or depth of feeling in response to expectable life stressors and challenges. This gives us a much more accurate picture of a disorder than simply looking at symptoms, such as having depressed feelings or losing one's appetite; these symptoms, in and of themselves, are a different matter than the quality of a person's feelings and experiences, such as the absence of joy and the presence of actual sadness most of the time.

Thought Disorders

As we look at this broad definition of mental health disorders we can see how the different types of traditionally described disorders fit in. When, for example, there is a deficit in the ability to connect ideas together and think logically, we have the basis for a thought disorder. This could occur at two levels: The first is when the person just can't think logically; the other—even more fundamental—is when the person doesn't have the sense of how one event or one experience causes another, which is an ability that normally develops even earlier than does our ability to use ideas.

The understanding of causality is based on experience of how the world works (for example, "My smile leads to a smile from you."). The person who doesn't have a sense of that has a thought disorder, often associated with a vulnerability to unrealistic thinking. In this case there may be delusions or hallucinations or faulty reality testing—in which the person doesn't know the real from the unreal—and there may be behavior based on lack of appreciation of reality. Included under the term "thought disorders" are terms such as "schizophrenia" or "psychosis." Borderline conditions, also called "borderline personality disorders," reflect a less severe deficit: the person can sometimes be realistic, but under stress becomes unrealistic in his thinking and shows problems with organizing his thoughts.

Then, depending on the constrictions in the range of feelings, the depth of feelings, and the stability of feelings the person can experience, we get into the different personality disorders: passive-dependent, passive-aggressive, avoidant, aggressive, or narcissistic. Even what are sometimes called "schizoid" or "paranoid" personality disorders suggest an extreme constriction in the range, depth, and stability of feelings, to the extent that it interferes with aspects of reality testing and the separation of reality of fantasy.

Limited Disorders

Then we have groups of disorders that are more limited in their scope, such as anxiety disorders and phobias. The person with one of these disorders can function reasonably well, but has areas of extreme fear, panic, or anxiety, and an inability to successfully negotiate certain feelings. Therefore, the fearful and phobic person often has trouble with anger and assertiveness, and is constricted in his emotional range or doesn't have stability of this range when it comes to the whole angry side of life. Or we can have a person who gets depressed, but not to such a degree that it interferes with reality testing. That person may have a predominant focus on negative feelings and difficulty with experiencing happiness, assertiveness, and a sense of mastery.

One of the principles of this kind of disorder is that, often, when there is a constriction in the range of feelings—a limitation in certain feelings—there is an exaggeration of other feelings. For each of the more encapsulated, or limited, patterns of symptoms—those that involve only moderate to mild constriction—there are various degrees of limitation in the range, depth, or stability of certain feelings, leading to the exaggeration of other feelings. Sometimes, it's behavior that becomes exaggerated—for example, the lack of true caring about others or the lack of the ability to restrain oneself may result in episodic impulsivity. The person whose feelings are superficial, who doesn't have full depth of feeling, may wind up being very self-centered and therefore have mild to moderate narcissistic tendencies.

So in this way of looking at mental health disorders, we look not simply at the symptom pattern, but at the person's behavior, feelings, and relationships in the context of what we think of as ideal or optimal mental health; then we look at the degree of mental illness, in terms of whether it's a deficit or constriction; and finally we determine whether it's a major constriction or a moderate to mild constriction.

This framework lends itself well to our developmental bio-psycho-social model, which is exemplified by the DIR model (also known as the DIR/Floortime Model because of the importance of unstructured interaction, or "Floortime," in the treatment prescribed). We can also apply the DIR model to the broad range of mental health challenges and mental health disorders, but we can also apply the techniques in simply listening more closely to people in our families or communities. The DIR model approach can work beautifully when dealing with such prickly individuals as the teenager in the house or the "difficult person in the office." Once we've looked at deficits and constrictions, rather than just at symptoms, we can then look at each of the common mental health problems and use our developmental lens to see how that problem indicates a deviation from the age-appropriate developmental milestones we expect in typical development. Then we assess what kind of deviation (or deficit) the person has, and whether it is severe, moderate, or mild. When we do that, the principles by which we can prevent a mental health disorder from occurring, or work toward overcoming a disorder that is already present, become clearer, as do the ways we can strengthen mental health in general. This enables us to help patch the individual's inner security blanket.

To illustrate the DIR model, the following chapters will look at the kinds of environments that support healthy mental and emotional development, as well as the importance of non-verbal communication, and specific types of disorders, beginning with anxiety and depression. We also consider how to accomplish our prevention and mastery goals. Finally, we address the more severe thought disorders and personality disorders and other common mental health issues.

Chapter 2

Environments That Support Emotional Development

The overarching term "environment" refers to the life experiences, family patterns, and relationships that support healthy functioning and help individuals overcome mental health disorders or prevent those disorders from developing in the first place. Several general characteristics are important in the environments of people who have or have tendencies toward any type of mental health problem. These characteristics are present in the home, school, work, or recreational environments, as appropriate for the age of the individual.

Author and environmentalist Bill McKibben describes the difficulties we live with today in these terms:

> The work begun by the Reformation was finished by fossil fuel, which freed farmers from the land, liberated us from days of manual labor, and granted us a mobility that expanded human horizons. People moved. . . All of these liberations have brought benefit, often greater benefit: they have helped produce the ideas we hold dearest, such as democracy; they helped spur the civil rights and women's revolutions; and they have made us much, much richer. But most of them carried costs, sometimes harder for us to see. We surrendered a fixed identity—a community, an extended family, deep and comforting roots—for, quite literally, the "chance to make something of ourselves.". . . This liberation is exhilarating, and it is daunting; it is exciting, and it is lonely. (p. 96)

The loss of the deep comforting roots of an extended family and community contribute not only to loneliness, the loss can also contribute to several mental health issues and the general unraveling of one's inner security blanket. This chapter addresses the ways in which we can build—or rebuild—a supportive community.

Characteristics of Supportive Environments and Communities

1. They Are Regulating

First, the environment should be very regulating in a way that is tailored to the specific needs of the child or adult. By "regulating," we mean paying attention to the key elements that stress or calm and comfort a person. The key is to remember that what is regulating for one person may not be so for another—it all depends on the person's unique mental and physical profile. For example, individuals who experience a lot of stress and anxiety and are irritable—or even individuals who may be out of touch with reality in terms of their beliefs or their perceptual experiences—are often easily overwhelmed. Such people need a calm, gentle, soothing environment. To create this kind of environment, we want to counter-regulate with our behavior and the way the environment is set up. If an individual is irritable or overloaded, we have to be calm and soothing when we interact with him, and we want to minimize overly-stimulating sounds, lights, activities, and so forth. The tendency, unfortunately, is often to throw fuel on the fire: when someone gets anxious, it makes others around him anxious; it becomes contagious, and then the whole atmosphere becomes unregulated and tense. So we want to be very careful that this doesn't happen.

On the other hand, there are people who are more depressed and lethargic, or who tend to retreat into a fantasy world. What is regulating for them is to be drawn into a shared world, where they are part of what is happening, where they are aware of and participate in the sights, the sounds, and the activities of others in the overall physical environment. However, this has to be done in a very gradual and respectful way so they don't get frightened and overwhelmed, which just causes them to retreat again. They need more energy, but not an anxious, urgent energy. So, if a child is off in a corner reading all the time, we don't want to grab her and say, "Hey! Come on! We're playing Tag and you're it!!"

Or if a woman is very withdrawn and just stays home watching TV, we don't want to drag her out to a busy mall to go shopping.

The way to draw people like this out is to pay attention to their interests and build on those interests. For example, when a person is very self-absorbed and lost in his own world and maybe only finds comfort in computer games, the computer game itself may be the way to approach him. It can be done very gradually, by asking about the avatars, taking turns playing it with him, or asking him to teach you how to play it. In this way, we slowly foster a little more interaction with the environment. We want to gradually help him get used to interacting with people to begin the process of getting him more regulated.

Now, it's important not to fall into the trap of thinking that if someone is sitting quietly, doing her own thing all the time, then she is regulated, because she appears so calm. Good regulation does not mean retreating into one's own world all the time, because the person who retreats can get overwhelmed by her inner world, and not have any balance with the external world. Some quiet, alone time is normal and healthy; when it's a person's default setting and she has trouble interacting with others, that's when she needs to be drawn out.

So, the first characteristic of environments that encourage mental health for people is that they be regulating and tailored to the specific needs of the person involved. Indeed, we all can use some accommodation from the people around us to be the happiest and healthiest we can be.

2. There Is Warm Interaction and Engagement

The second characteristic of environments that help people make progress in terms of their mental health challenges is that they provide human relationships and engagement—that there is always some opportunity to form warm, pleasurable, respectful, and more intimate relationships. Families, obviously, can provide this characteristic best (except very dysfunctional families), but schools, work, and recreational environments can also provide it.

This characteristic, too, should be tailored to the needs of the individual. For example, a child with behavioral disorders, who has been shifted around quite a bit from one foster care situation to another, may require an educational setting where he can have the same teacher for a number of years, so that he doesn't have to lose the teacher like he's lost foster parents over and over again. A person who is very self-absorbed and who gets caught up in her own obsessive-compulsive rituals may need to be pulled into relationships very gradually, otherwise she'll feel overwhelmed and will retreat. A person who is anxious, clingy, and dependent may easily form relationships, but the relationships will be very need-based. For this kind of person, the engagement should provide a little more balance. He needs help him being a little more sensitive to others' needs while also taking a little more initiative and becoming more independent—so he learns how to have two-way relationships.

Bill McKibben writes at length about the environmental value of shopping locally and avoiding big box stores, but his concept also applies to relationship building as we mean it. He writes,

> ...sociologists studying shopping behavior reported recently that consumers have *ten times as many conversations* at farmers' markets as they do at supermarkets. A simple change in economic life—where you shop—produces an enormous change in your social life. You go from being a mere consumer to being a participant, talking about what you like and dislike, expanding your sense of who's in your community and how it fits together. (p. 105-106)

A change in relationship life, so to speak, can make an enormous impact on an individual's mental health. For example, the way to engineer a two-way relationship with a very dependent person, is that, as we empathize and listen, we also try to reciprocate and share a little bit in conversation. That makes it more of a real relationship, as opposed to a typical therapeutic relationship in which the therapist keeps some anonymity and it's all about the patient. This helps the individual learn to take an interest in another person and not always be the center of attention. The process needs to be done very gradually, particularly for the person who has trouble holding onto reality, because he may get overwhelmed if you share too much or demand too much attention too quickly.

The person who is depressed or withdrawn, on the other hand, needs more wooing to be pulled into a relationship. And someone who is impulsive and exploits people, treating others like objects and moving from one relationship to another very quickly, may need a long time to learn to be warm, empathetic, and intimate. With this kind of person, we have to be very patient and provide a consistent relationship, even if he is constantly sabotaging it by making you feel unimportant, exploited, or like a chair or table rather than another human being. Eventually, we can probably work our way into his heart and become a real person to him, but it may require months or maybe even years of patience, empathy, and warmth before we sense that kernel of real affection emerging. Obviously, this is a choice we are more likely to make with a family member than a work colleague, and this kind of person will need professional therapy as well.

3. They Explore the Full Range of Emotions

The third characteristic of an environment that promotes mental health is that it helps the individual explore, experience, understand, and communicate the different emotions of life. Human beings are basically emotional creatures; we have a seemingly infinite variety of emotions, because each emotion—anger, sadness, joy, contentment, competitiveness, sorrow, curiosity, and so forth—has infinite shades to it. If we understand our feelings, we can describe them in a million different ways, and this is good therapy (whether with a therapist, a loved one, or the guy at the produce stand). But we can't understand and describe our feelings until we can experience them. Then, the more subtly we experience our feelings, the more easily we can communicate them, work with them, and learn to cope with them.

Learning to experience feelings and recognize them in others develops from two-way emotional communication, which includes facial expressions and gestures as well as words. Thus, we want our healing relationships and environments to have lots of back-and-forth interaction in which emotional expressions and eventually emotional descriptions are being exchanged; not in a cross-examining way, or in an interviewing way, or in an upsetting way, but in an empathetic way. As family members, teachers, therapists, or friends become animated responders, tuning in expressively—with eyes, with gestures, with soothing vocalizations—to how the individual is feeling, that person feels recognized, before words are even used.

In other words, if an individual is anxious and frantic, and someone listens to him calmly, with a facial expression and gestures that convey real understanding and warmth—without either dismissing or exaggerating his anxiety, but with a nice, middle ground of concern and reassurance—the individual's feeling experience is affirmed. As someone does this for the individual's full range of feelings, he becomes more comfortable in experiencing (and expressing) different feelings. This can be a gradual process of growth: through this kind of relationship, as an inkling of a feeling emerges and then gets acknowledged by the other person, there is a gradual expansion in the range of feelings over many weeks, months, or even years.

We can also create situations in which an individual can experience new feelings. If someone never seems joyful, we try to find activities of interest to him, in which he can begin to feel pleasure. If someone never asserts himself, never takes the initiative, we can encourage this by setting up a situation in which he has to make a decision about which option he wants, or, if it's a child, has to ask someone to move so he can go outside, for example. We can also create situations in which that person does something for someone else, even if it's as simple as giving another person an apple. Then he will experience the feelings that go along with acts of kindness, and see the counter-response: a smile, a warm "Thank you!" and perhaps a hug. Experiencing the counter-response is a very important component of developing a full range of feelings.

For many people with mental health problems, the full range of feelings is scary. For the anxious person, aggression is often scary. For the depressed, self-absorbed person, assertiveness and competition may be scary. For the person who is very impulsive or self-centered (sometimes called narcissistic), true intimacy and warmth may be scary. So it's very important that, as we help an individual to experience new feelings, we do it gradually and slowly so the new feeling doesn't overwhelm him. A compulsive person, who has a very narrow range of feelings and likes to control everything with rituals, is going to need a particularly slow, step-by-step process; we need to approach him through his interests and then gradually expand the range of feelings around those interests. Expanding the range of feelings is very important for helping people overcome mental health problems, because—for various reasons (biological and/or psychological)—these individuals have not had opportunities to develop the full range of feelings and flexible coping strategies for their feelings.

The key is to keep expanding the emotional range, while tailoring the process to the specific needs of the individual. There is no substitute for empathy and understanding in your facial expressions, and reflecting the mood and emotion of the person you are talking with, and then gradually trying to provide experiences that expand the emotion a little bit. The other important aspect is to make the exchange more reciprocal in the sense that the person learns to understand our emotional responses as well. The best way to help someone do this is to be animated in our expressions; he will experience us as other individuals through our empathy first, and then through our reactions to him.

As we help the person expand their emotional range we should always be ready to counter-regulate. For example, if a person becomes agitated and upset, we should be very soothing. If a person is very lethargic, be a little more energizing. If the person is very impulsive, be a little more containing. If the person is fragmented, try to be a little more organized.

4. They Encourage the Use of Creative and Logical Expressions of Emotions

The next characteristic of environments that promote mental health is that they encourage the individual's ability to form ideas related to feelings, and the verbal expression of emotions, in both creative and logical ways.

In the creative arena, we can encourage children to express the full range of human drama in pretend play—dolls or stuffed animals can hug or fight or compete or feed each other, for example—gently helping them to explore the emotions with which they are uncomfortable. With older children, adolescents, and even adults, we can promote the creative expression of emotional ideas through artistic endeavors such as creating plays, shooting short films on DVD cameras, writing short stories, drawing or other visual art, or sculpture.

The creative realm allows an individual to learn about, experience, and express the world of feelings in ways that don't have to conform to reality or to problem-solving efforts. For example, a child can create a scenario in which he has all the toys he wants, or has his own house that his sister can't enter without his permission; an adult can write out a story about all the successes she wants, or how she would get even with those who annoy her. The key is to respect all of the individual's ideas and expressions of feelings, to begin where the person is and expand from there. For children who start off being aggressive in their play, if we are empathetic and play along with that, eventually the pretend drama will develop themes of nurturing and warmth. For example, a doll will take care of a sick teddy bear, whereas if we try to direct the child away from the aggression without letting it play out, she will have a harder time moving beyond it.

Then, moving into the logical use of ideas about feelings, we want to help the individual to describe the feelings symbolically, because this allows him to discuss his feelings and problem-solve around them. For example, if a man needs more affection, he can express that to his spouse; a child can tell mommy or daddy that he needs to have a night-light on to fall asleep. If a person is angry, she can express how angry she feels with words, without having to act on it or suppress it. Developing the ability to put feelings into symbols (words or pictures) means that one doesn't have to act on impulse; one can explore and express feelings that shouldn't be acted on, such as rage, aggression, excessive neediness, or despair.

As a family member, friend, teacher, or colleague, your empathy for the logical expression of feelings such as anger, selfishness, and other "negative" emotions will eventually help an individual to express warmth and concern, as well as feelings of vulnerability and dependency and concerns about getting needs met. You don't have to push this process, just let it occur gradually. If you are a family member, you are not "playing therapist," you are simply creating an atmosphere where these expressions can emerge naturally.

So, encouraging expression of the full range of feelings through ideas is the critical fourth characteristic of environments that help individuals overcome mental health challenges. Again, this process has to be sensitive to individual differences: the anxious person is going to have a lot of ideas about his security needs, about needing you to help him calm down, about reassurance—the child wants to be told 100 times that robbers won't come in at night and kidnap him. The man who is worried when his wife goes away on a business trip wants the same type of reassurance. But, rather than offering reassurance too quickly, listen and empathize and help the person become better at expressing his feelings, more elaborate in his descriptions. That is the key, and that becomes reassuring in its own right. Then the reassurance about the particular fear can come at the end. Essayist Anne Lamott puts this beautifully, describing a painful incident in her past, ". . . it had made my heart ache over the years. I did not explain or justify my triggers—the jealousy especially, because trigger implies weapons, weapons take aim, aim implies combat, combat implies engagement. All I wanted was to feel less engaged, less stuck: I wanted to let it go, which is *so* not my strong suit, any more than forgiveness is. . . But I felt scared." (p. 115)

All of us—as family members, friends, teachers, or even therapists of people with mental health challenges—have buttons that get pushed around certain feelings, so we are less empathetic or tuned-in to some feelings than others. But it's very important to learn how to tune in to all the feelings; as we're helping the individual broaden her range of feelings, we can do the same with ourselves. If an individual is depressed, for example, we may be uncomfortable with his implicit neediness, or scared of his sadness, or the depths of his despair may touch on feelings we have that we don't like to look at. But being aware of that while we listen and empathize helps us tune in, which makes us more helpful. Through our empathy, our concern, our listening, our occasional non-intrusive but clarifying or amplifying question, we can help someone become a "poet of his feelings," which is very, very helpful. Anne Lamott continues with, "But I finally, finally forgive me; sort of-ish. No curtain of light or soft angel voices, but the understanding that forgiving myself makes it possible to forgive them, too. . . and it feels as if someone finally cracked open a window that had been jammed." (p. 116)

Points to Remember

Environments that support emotional development:

- Are very regulating in a way that is tailored to the specific needs of the child or adult.
- Provide opportunities to form warm, pleasurable, respectful, and more intimate relationships.
- Help the individual explore, experience, understand, and communicate the different emotions of life.
- Encourage the individual's ability to form ideas related to feelings, and the verbal expression of emotions, in both creative and logical ways.

As family members, friends, therapists, or colleagues of people with mental health challenges, we want to interact in a empathetic, supportive way, gently encouraging the other person to express themselves, while at the same time becoming aware of our own "buttons" or issues.

In the next chapter, we look at how specific environments and experiences can make individuals with mental health challenges move from basic logical thinking to making sense of their inner world, and then on to the higher levels of thinking.

Chapter 3

Environments That Support Higher Levels of Thinking

Home, school, work, and recreational environments can also provide experiences and relationships that help individuals with mental health challenges to move beyond the stages described earlier, and learn to make sense of and get perspective on their internal worlds. From there, they can move on to higher levels of thinking. Let's look at that process in depth.

Making Sense of the Internal World

We want to help individuals with mental health challenges understand why they are angry, sad, needy, scared, anxious, impulsive, and so forth. This is no easy task in any environment, but some families focus on it as a matter of course more than other families do. In some families, for example, if a child says she wants to go outside, the parent naturally asks, "Why? What do you want to do?" The "why" stirs up a reflective attitude that makes the child want to understand things, including herself. In other families, the parent just answers "Yes" or "No," which doesn't encourage reflection.

Similarly, if the child is looking sad, rather than saying something like, "Cheer up! You have nothing to be glum about," which hardly gets at the causes of things, a parent can ask, "Why so glum today, Sweetheart? What happened?" or, "Gee, it looks like something has made you unhappy today," and so forth. The same principle applies to teenagers and adults. You don't have to ask an intrusive question, you can just comment, "Boy, it looks like today was a rough day" or "…a great day," opening the door to more dialogue that leads to understanding and making sense of thoughts and feelings.

1. Encouraging Logical Connections

Always work with the person to help them make sense of their internal world. Of course, this is particularly hard to do with people who are being unrealistic or illogical, but they need more sense-making discussions than anyone else. The person may be blaming others for the whole situation—"My teacher was unfair to me," or "That jerk cut me off," or "Samantha won't share any of her toys with me"—with no acknowledgement of the role that she herself might be playing. In these cases, it's tempting to say something like, "Well, you didn't finish your homework," or "You were in the wrong lane," or "Last time you and Samantha played together, you broke her favorite doll," to get the person to take responsibility. But it's important to first understand why she feels it's necessary to blame others.

You can say things like, "Gee, it sounds like a lot of people were mean today. What do you think was going on?" That gets the person curious. Then, gradually, over many weeks or months, as you acknowledge the way she views the world, ask her to look at the bigger picture with you: "How come they were all so mean today, do you think?" "I don't know, I don't care, I just want them to be nice." "Did they all wake up on the wrong side of the bed?" Eventually the person will start asking herself, "Gee, is there something I do that puts people off, that makes people be so unfair to me? Did I do something to make that happen?"

If you're a family member, you don't want to play therapist, but just gradually encourage the person to be reflective. It starts with very basic interactions. For example, if someone tends to wander from topic to topic and goes off on tangents that don't seem to relate, start by amplifying and clarifying the lack of structure: "Wait, I'm confused. You were telling me about A and now you're talking about C and now about F—I'm lost here." Let the person do the clarifying. This is especially important for children, but is also helpful for adults who go off on tangents in their discussions. You want to help the person "connect the dots" when she seems to get off on tangents; often the thoughts are connected in the person's mind on some level, and you can help her think about how A and C relate.

For example, the person might be talking about being disappointed at work, and then all of a sudden jump to describing a movie she saw. You may realize that this new thought might be actually continuing the theme; the movie may have to do with someone who was very successful and is treated in a way that the person wishes she were treated. But you don't want to suggest that; you just want to supportively, empathetically encourage the person to make the connection herself. Once you build the structure of logic through the use of words, pictures, or other symbols, then you can gradually apply it to the world of feelings.

Recognize that everyone with mental health challenges has different feelings about which they can't be logical, because of their particular mental health problem: the anxious person may be quite logical about feeling A, such as being sad, but not about feeling B, such as feeling panicked. We all have holes in our logic in the areas where we have our problems; that is part of the reason why we have the problems. So don't expect the person who you are trying to help to be equally logical in all areas. In fact, look for illogic in the areas where her problems are, whether it's her fears (any dog will attack her), her depression (she's convinced that nothing will ever get better), or her need for ritualized behavior (unless she washes the door three times, something terrible will happen). You have to respect the person's own sense of logic about the situation, starting with empathy and verbalization, and then help her look at the situation in comparison to other areas in which she actually is more logical. The person who is impulsive or self-centered has a logic that seems illogical to most, which is that she can't trust people. Well, eventually she may let you know that she has good reason for that feeling or that belief.

So, helping people to make logical sense of the world and stay reality-based is another characteristic of environments that promote mental health. Again, this is done by tailoring the interactions to the needs of the individual and gradually and empathetically promoting the exploration of feelings and creativity. In other words, an advice-giving role with practical problem-solving suggestions can be counter-productive to helping the individual develop these skills. Rather, being understanding and empathizing through facial expressions, the eyes, gestures, and helping the person summarize and express what she's feeling creates a healthy environment.

However, you don't want to overdo it by responding to every comment with, for example, "Well, why do you feel that way?" Rather, if a theme is emerging in the conversation, or the person's tone of voice suggests a justified (at least from her point of view, even if you don't agree) feeling of disappointment, regret, anger, outrage, or suspiciousness, you can ask a question that conveys your understanding that she has a good reason for feeling that way. For example, you can simply ask, "Did anything upsetting happen today?" The person may not initially be aware of a connection between something that happened—such as another kid being mean to her on the playground or daddy not coming home as early as he promised, or, if it's an adult, something as simple as having to wait a long time for the bus after work—and her feelings. Sometimes people are embarrassed to admit even to themselves that something simple and seemingly unimportant has upset them, but if you, by your question, indicate that there may be a good reason for the person's feelings, you can help her to make sense of her thoughts and feelings to a greater degree by exploring reasons for them. This process begins opening the door to higher levels of thinking, discussed below.

2. Encouraging Multi-Causal Thinking

When the individual can establish a causal connection between feelings and events or ideas, the next step is to help him look for more than one reason for feelings: "It sounds like that bus driver was really rude. Did anything else happen today that might contribute to the way you feel? Was everything okay at work?" The person may have experienced a series of little insults—each seemingly minor, but adding up. Or the reaction to the minor irritation may be a diversion from something bigger: perhaps he is actually worried about losing his job. We want to help him achieve multi-causal thinking in order to have a clearer, more complex understanding of the situation.

3. Encouraging Gray Area Thinking

Once a person can easily make sense of and explore multiple reasons for her feelings, we want to create experiences that foster an even higher level of thinking, one in which the world is looked at in shades of gray, known as gray-area thinking. So, rather than living in an all-or-nothing world where when we are upset, anxious, very angry, or depressed, we feel that everything is terrible, or everyone is mean or nobody pays enough attention to us, we can live in a world that's somewhat one way and somewhat another way. It has shades of gray. Most of us are capable of gray-area thinking, but not when we are upset or in the grip of extreme emotions. In a sense, the more we can use gray-area reasoning regarding our feelings, the more we experience feelings in gradations rather than as all-or-nothing calamities, the more mentally healthy we are. Rather than feeling overwhelmingly depressed, angry, or upset whenever something disturbs us, we can feel a little angry, a little sad, a little disappointed, a little annoyed, and so forth. Sometimes when a situation is very intense, our feelings do have that overwhelming, all-or-nothing, catastrophic quality. Again, we turn to Anne Lamott reflecting on her difficult relationship with her mother,

> I could forgive her only about half the time. I was struggling to learn the little things she forgot to teach me—that I was beautiful, and of value, regardless of how well or poorly I was doing in the world—and was mad that she had given me such a lousy owner's manual. . . When people reminisced about her, I would put my hand to my brow and shake my head slowly. "Ay-yi-yi," I always said. But now, a few years after her death, I can see in my son's eyes so many points I'd missed about her. (p. 88)

On the other hand, people with mental health problems often succumb to all-or-nothing, catastrophic feelings. When they are anxious, they think the world will come to an end or something terrible will happen to them or people they love; when they are depressed, they think they're terrible people and have no reason to go on living, and so forth. The ability for gray-area thinking when it comes to feelings actually helps people overcome many mental health disorders, including anxiety and depression, because it combats the tendency of these disorders to lock people into all-or-nothing feeling states. Once they can apply that ability to the intense feelings of life, they often make significant progress; this is one of the aspects of good therapy that's so helpful—talking about the subtleties and nuances and shades of feelings.

The environment that helps people overcome their mental health disorders is one in which we're always looking for opportunities to see shades of gray. One way to do this is with comparisons: "The depression you feel today—how does it compare to yesterday's depression? Is it a little bit more or a little bit less? How does it compare to the saddest day of your life?" The person might answer, "Well, this is the saddest day of my life; I've never felt so bad before." And then you can ask, "Well, do you think tomorrow will be even worse or the same?" Comparative thinking is a variation of gray-area thinking. When we're having these discussions with children, we sometimes have them show us with their hands how strong a certain feeling is: if their hands are close together, it's not very strong; if their hands are all the way apart, it's the worst the feeling's ever been, and so forth. Often, of course, you can tell from the person's facial expressions and vocal tone how strong the feeling is, but helping her express it—verbally and with gestures—can be very helpful; it helps the person put the feeling into context.

Gray-area thinking also supports big picture thinking—seeing the whole forest rather than just one tree or a few trees. In other words, it gives perspective: "Well, yes, this was disappointing, but compared to what could have happened…" or, "Yes, I was in a car accident and I did break my leg, but thank God I'm still alive and I'm going to heal and get back to the way I was." If we have the ability for gray-area thinking, then even events that are truly catastrophic are be easier to deal with; they are less overwhelming.

4. Encouraging Reflective Thinking

Environments that promote mental health also help people to achieve the next level of thinking, which is reflective thinking. This is the ability to think in two frames of reference at the same time, to say things like, "Gee, I'm angrier about the traffic today than I usually am—I wonder why." In other words, people with this ability have a stable sense of how they usually are, and then they can assess their current state in relation to the usual state; they can judge themselves. They can do this in their work, judging that they did better on one project than they did on another, but more importantly, they can do it in terms of their feeling world: "Today wasn't such a bad day, so why am I so depressed?" Or even, "Usually so-and-so really annoys me, but today he didn't bother me at all," or, "I'm normally a depressed kind of person, but today I feel kind of cheerful—I wonder why?" They can explore reasons for the way they feel, using a stable sense of how they normally are as a benchmark.

As that reflective ability expands, a person can project into the future: "I wonder how I'll feel about this tomorrow?" and can explore historical antecedents: not only what happened today to cause the feeling, but what in general makes her tend to feel depressed or anxious or angry. She can ask herself questions such as, "I wonder what happened in my childhood that makes me react this way?" or, "How am I contributing to my mood with what I'm doing or thinking?" or, "Why do I always get myself into hot water with my finances?"

At this level of self-reflection we can see our own patterns, compare them to the way we want to be or to some future goals that we may have ("It seems like the kids who are doing really well in school are more organized than I am; why am I so disorganized?"), look at the past, and try to make sense of everything together. This ability depends not only on intellectual skills, but on having a core sense of self, because it's the self—the "me"—who is making these comparisons and asking these questions. Once we have a core sense of self, then we can make comparisons to that self.

Often, therapy supports the development of this ability because the therapeutic process identifies some of our blind spots, the areas in which our anxieties and our upbringing contribute us to "taking our eye off the ball." We all have certain feelings we don't like to look at, such as humiliation, anger, competitiveness, jealousy, and so forth. By identifying those hidden or suppressed feelings, therapy helps us, often, to become more reflective, to broaden our reflective range. Good relationships with family members, friends, teachers, and colleagues can also help people do that, as long as they are empathetic, non-critical, and focused on understanding before problem-solving or trying to give advice. Better than giving advice is to help the individual come up with his own advice, his own solutions. Use simple questions that promote comparison and reflection: "How does how you feel today compare to how you usually feel?" "I wonder why today was such a tough day for you," and so forth. So, the final characteristic of environments that support mental health is that they promote this reflective attitude.

Points to Remember

Environments That Support Higher Levels of Thinking:

- Encourage the person to become more reality-based, make logical connections and make sense of their internal world.

- Are understanding and empathetic through facial expressions, gestures, and helping the person summarize and express what she is feeling.
- Help the person look for more than one reason for his feelings.
- Create experiences which encourage the person to see the world in shades of gray, a world that's somewhat one way and somewhat another way. Also, help the person compare how they are feeling today with how they felt before in similar situations. Comparative thinking is a variation of gray-area thinking.
- Help the person to do reflective thinking, the ability to think in two frames of reference at the same time. This ability helps the person have a stable sense of how they usually are, and assess their current state in relation to the usual state; they can judge themselves.

These attributes, along with those described in the previous chapter, give us a blueprint to follow when we want to help someone with mental health challenges. We all have our own issues that get in the way of implementing this ideal perfectly. But we can work toward this goal, and in the process help improve the mental health not only of the person we care about, but also our own mental health.

In summary, there are a number of critical attributes of environments that support mental health in general and also help people work toward overcoming specific mental health disorders. The environment has to be regulating, tailored to the individual's mental and physical profile, engaging, and interactive, and it should very gradually expand the person's experience of feelings and perception of other's feelings, the ability to verbalize feelings and be creative with feelings, the ability to make logical sense of feelings, and then the ability to do this at higher levels including giving multiple reasons for things, looking at shades of gray, and finally being able to be reflective. That's a tall order for an environment to provide, particularly when everyone else in the environment has their own limitations and their own problems. But it gives us something to strive for, a kind of blueprint. As family members, teachers, co-workers, therapists, and friends of someone with mental health challenges, we are all going to fall short of that blueprint because we are all going to have areas where we are not comfortable, and so we'll be inclined at times to give advice, rather than empathetically leading the person to figuring out the solution for himself. As author Anne Lamott wrote, "I realize what superhuman patience it took for my mother to live with kids. I see Sam [Lamott's son] and me get mad at each other, over and over, but then we apologize, become friends again; I see how each time this is redemption. How amazing it is to share that." (p. 89)

We can assess how well we are doing in terms of creating this kind of environment by asking ourselves a few simple questions: When do I stop being comforting and regulating? When do I lose it? When do I stop being empathetic and instead start giving advice or get into practical problem-solving or lecturing before I understand or let the person express herself? When do I lecture or tell her what to do rather than helping her figure it out for herself? When do I look for quick and easy fixes—all-or-nothing answers—rather than promoting gray-area thinking? When do I resort to an overly simplistic solution rather than looking for truly reflective understanding of the situation at hand? As we ask ourselves these questions, and learn from the answers we discover, we can make a big positive difference in the life of any family member, friend, student, or colleague who is having a mental health problem, while expanding our own mental health in the process.

Chapter 4

The Importance of Non-Verbal Communication

In working with adults and children with any mental and emotional challenges, we need to keep in mind the importance of non-verbal, or pre-symbolic, communication. By non-verbal or pre-symbolic communication, we mean behaviors such as head nods, smiles, smirks, tone of voice, hand motions, body posture, raising of the eyebrows, and so forth.

Why are these so important? After all, we are verbal, symbolic people. Most of us tend to think in words or visual symbols. But imagine that you are walking down a dark alley at night and a stranger comes up to you. He has a menacing look on his face, but says, "Don't worry, you can trust me, I just need some directions." We'd be likely to run away, or certainly we'd feel nervous about interacting with him. On the other hand, if a person with a sweet smile comes your way looking kind of helpless, and indicates that they need help, you are likely to be kind and helpful, or at least feel secure, even if they don't speak English and we can't understand their words. The suspicious side of us may still be suspicious, but we won't be nearly as anxious as with the first person.

So, we trust people's non-verbal communication, even more than we trust the words that people use. If someone smiles at us and says something a little off-color, we are likely to forgive her. But if someone says, "Oh, you look wonderful," but shakes her head disapprovingly and has a critical tone of voice, we are likely to think she is a phony. When we see politicians on TV, we are always scrutinizing the degree to which their tone of voice or facial expression jives with their messages, which is why politicians go through hours and hours of coaching. Similarly, good actors have the ability to use their tone of voice and their non-verbal communication to get into character.

It's easier to trust the non-verbal system of communication than the verbal system, and actually there's a good reason for that: it comes earlier in our development. In the first six stages of development, babies first learn how to pay attention, then how to calm down, then they begin to engage with others, and then they learn the simple forms of non-verbal communication—taking an object from a parent's hand, giving it back, smiling and making little sounds back-and-forth with a caregiver. These kinds of exchanges constitute the first stage of non-verbal communication, or "two-way communication."

Next comes the stage of what we call "shared social problem-solving" in which the toddler gets into a continuous flow of back-and-forth interaction, such as taking a parent by the hand, walking the parent to the refrigerator, pointing to the food that he wants, nodding yes when the parent takes out the right juice, nodding no when the parent takes out the wrong juice, and so forth. There is a whole dialogue going on non-verbally, as the parent and the child solve problems together, whether it be getting juice, finding the toy the child wants, or whatever. So when we refer to non-verbal, pre-symbolic communication, we mean this collage of non-verbal interactions orchestrated to solve problems, in addition to the earlier stage of basic two-way communication. Some children begin to use a few words at this time too, but this is just a minor aspect of the communication system; it won't become more dominant until the child is closer to 18 months of age, and usually it does not become the primary way of communicating until the child is two or three.

What is notable, however, is that the non-verbal system continues to be very important throughout life, long after symbols become predominant. So we have, in essence, several ways of communicating. They are often synchronized together, and when someone appears believable, the non-verbal and verbal systems agree. They complement each other. If someone says, "I love you," or "I like you," and the tone of voice and the facial expression convey an appropriate level of warmth, we believe the person. It is very different to hear a computer-generated voice on an answering machine—"please... leave... a... message"—than to hear a warm, live body saying, "Oh, so-and-so would love to speak to you, can he call you back this evening?" These are very different messages, with very different effects on the person calling.

Thus, the non-verbal system is important in all communication. But it also has specific importance to how we work with children and adults with mental and emotional challenges. As described above, the first type of non-verbal communication is basic two-way communication, which establishes the first sense of reality—the first sense that there is something inside me (a desire, an impulse) that communicates with someone or something outside me.

The sense of reality begins from day one, as the baby attends to the outside world, and certainly when the baby engages with caregivers. But it is through predictable back-and-forth communication with that outside world (a smile begets a smile; a sound begets a sound) that an infant develops the beginning of causal thinking and a sense of how reality works. It also helps to further establish a boundary between what is inside the infant and what is outside the infant; the sense of self is beginning to form. The beginning of a sense of "me" or a sense of self and a sense of "you" forms through the fact that the baby smiles and mother smiles back. And it is also the beginning of the sense of will, of taking an action to get a desired result. The baby grabs a toy because he knows it will make a sound, for example. Predictable feedback to an action—as opposed to random or chaotic feedback—helps establish a sense of self and of reality.

Thus, our first sense of self is non-verbal. This can occur simply through the exchange of smiles, but that creates a very narrow or limited sense of self. When it also occurs through protests—the baby makes a "Grrr!" sound when he is mad and frustrated, mother responds with, "Oh, Sweetheart, I'll be there in a second"—then the baby's sense of self includes being assertive. As long as the response to a baby's anger doesn't frighten him, then he can experience his own anger as part of himself. As time goes on, the baby develops a sense of himself that includes being sweet and happy, assertive, angry, scared (a stranger comes into the room and the baby looks frightened, and his mother responds with a reassuring hug), and so forth.

Every time a different emotion, intent, or motor pattern gets a response, the sense of self expands. That process typically occurs between four and 10 months of life. But for many children it occurs later, or occurs incompletely, and they grow into adults with a narrowly defined sense of self. They may have had a parent who only liked to interact with them when they were happy, not when they were sad or angry. Or, the parents only responded positively when the child was being compliant, not assertive. So, as adults, their sense of self doesn't include a comfortable sense of assertiveness, or a comfortable sense of expressing anger, or even a comfortable sense of curiosity or exploration. A fuller sense of self can be developed in the adult years, with appropriate therapy. But the limitation begins in the non-verbal system.

That same set of limitations can occur in phase two of non-verbal communication—the stage of shared social problem-solving. In this stage we establish the sense of self around the different emotional themes of life. We develop a repertoire of expressions and gestures: gestures that express closeness, dependency, happiness (big smiles, hugs), assertiveness, fear, anger (growls and grimaces), and so forth. So even without words, we have and express an emotional experience, and our sense of self becomes defined by our range of emotions. Is it a full range, or a shallow, constricted range?

What happens if we never get feedback for assertiveness, if, in fact, when we were assertive or angry, our caretaker froze and we experienced no feedback? Instead of getting reassuring words, gestures, sounds, or movements of any kind, we just got ignored or misread—maybe we were fussing because we wanted a toy, but instead our caregiver put a pacifier in our mouth. Lack of response or an inappropriate response didn't help further define what we were feeling inside; instead, we may have just felt confused or misunderstood.

Expanding the Range of Feelings in Adulthood

As an adult in therapy, if we try to explore that experience with the therapist only verbally—our feelings of confusion and anxiety around expressing anger or assertiveness—we're not likely to make very rapid progress, though just the awareness that that is a troublesome area helps a bit. But, on the other hand, if we have a therapist who works with that nonverbal system, who responds to our vocal tone of anger with an appropriate vocal tone of her own—whether it be a soothing or firm tone, we can begin to define our sense of self nonverbally even as an adult. It's never too late to broaden our sense of self. The key is having a therapist who works at the nonverbal level as well as the verbal level, and provides reciprocal feedback. We need these back-and-forth interactions around all the different emotional themes of life with subtle variations in tone of voice, body posture, and facial expression to stitch up a tattered inner security blanket. This often comes naturally with gifted therapists, but they need to be aware of what they are doing and aware of the systems that are not yet a part of the patient's nonverbal sense of self.

Then, in addition, the therapist can talk with the patient about the patient's experience of those emotional realms that aren't a part of his sense of self. Often, these emotions just get experienced as diffused anxiety, or the patient acts out or behaves in ways he doesn't understand, because the emotion is not yet a part of a gestural system, so it can't be identified symbolically. The patient may also misread his own and other people's feelings. His tone of voice is angry, but he says, "I feel fine." For the person who is too scared to explore assertiveness or anger directly, the therapist may look for opportunities when the emotion is fleetingly revealed and then respond very quickly to it in a nonverbal way, as well as drawing the patient's attention to it verbally: "Wait a second—you just gave me a funny little look. What was that?" Any shift in vocal tone, whether it's supportive or more assertive, gives the patient some feedback. Slowly, the patient begins to recognize these subtle emotional shifts on his own, and his sense of self will broaden.

In the next stage, the therapist and patient can explore the meanings the patient gives the emotion. Beginning when a child becomes symbolic (typically, in the second year of life), and learns to elaborate—to pretend play through words, and then through each of the following stages of connecting ideas together, answering "why" questions, and multi-causal, gray-area, and reflective thinking—he is always building on the nonverbal system. He is giving symbolic expression to what he already feels in his body. But he can only express what is already part of his sense of self. So if he never experiences assertiveness or anger or fear, for example, as part of his sense of self, it is hard for him to express it symbolically through the different developmental stages—to give multiple reasons for the feeling, or to reflect on it, for instance.

Thus, it is very important for all individuals with mental health problems to work on the nonverbal system. Depression often relates to difficulty with expressing anger or assertiveness. Anxiety often relates to difficulty with expressing fear or apprehension. Many mental health problems emanate from difficulty with expressing feelings of closeness and dependency.

The other side of the coin in terms of the nonverbal system relates to how we define others. Just as we develop an image or sense of ourselves, we also develop an image of others. Not only do we want to have a full sense of self, incorporating many different emotions, we can be loving, close, and happy, as well as fearful, assertive, and angry, but we want to perceive others in the same way, rather than seeing them as all one way or the other—all good or all bad. Do we have a balanced, full view of ourselves and of others that makes for an accurate understanding of the world? Of course, we may not see all aspects in every person, but we don't want to be limited in our perception.

Yet another important aspect of the nonverbal system is that it enables us to communicate, modulate, regulate, and control our emotions. Ordinarily, a 14-month-old toddler can express his anger with a tone of voice or a facial expression before he bites or pinches or knocks something over. Now, what determines whether that toddler becomes a child who is impulsive and aggressive, or a child who develops the capacity to say, "Mommy, I'm mad!" and uses his words instead of acting out? Well, if that toddler, as he begins to look a little annoyed because he can't reach a toy he wants, has a caregiver who says with a reassuring tone of voice, "Ohhhh! My sweetheart is getting annoyed! What can I do?"—recognizing the annoyance or frustration that is coming into the toddler's voice—that toddler now has sense of self that includes expressing annoyance through a gesture.

Then, if the parent brings the toy a little closer before the anger overflows, and the toddler can assert himself and reach for it, the toddler learns an important lesson: gesturing can lead to communication which can help him solve a problem before he has a tantrum. This toddler becomes a can-do, assertive child, who eventually is able to label or find words for his internal feelings; the symbolic system gives voice to the feelings that are already there nonverbally. By the time he develops words, he already knows how the world works. He knows all about anger, sadness, closeness, and scary feelings, in addition to knowing about objects such as food, or a chair, or a ball.

Thus, the nonverbal system helps us regulate and negotiate our emotions instead of acting them out, or just shutting down and withdrawing. A toddler has three choices: learning to gesture around all the different emotions (closeness with a big smile, reaching out his arms to be picked up, anger with an angry growl and facial expression, and so forth), putting the emotions into behavior (biting, grabbing, hitting, crying, or freezing up), or withdrawing. As a side note, children with special needs tend to either become impulsive and disorganized, or to withdraw. If we don't help them to develop the nonverbal system of communication and go right to trying to help them express words, they can become very mechanical or rote in their acquisition of words. This applies to our discussion of working with Asperger's Syndrome in this book's final chapter.

To help a child develop a healthy communication system and a healthy sense of self, we need to go through this nonverbal system. We do this by entering the child's world through back-and-forth interactions. The idea is to help the child to *want* to engage with us by making ourselves appealing and fun, finding a tone of voice that engages the child without overwhelming him, joining the child in his interests and activities, trying to get interactions going. Through these interactions, the child develops his gestural ability, and we help him develop it by responding to it. We want to get as many circles of communication (back-and-forth interactions) going as we can, while counter-balancing the child's emotions. If the child is angry, we become soothing; if he is impassive, we become more enticing and activating; if he is overwhelmed, we become calming. Thus, we are not only responding with different gestures, our gestures are helping him regulate his gestures by providing a counterbalancing system.

At the same time, we want to convey that we understand and respect the child's emotion. So, if the toddler is angry and shaking his fists, we might first join him in that gesture, while saying (in a much lighter tone of voice), "Oh! I know you're mad!" We're showing that we understand his anger, but at the same time we are being counterbalancing because our mimicking has warmth and calmness to it. Then, in a soothing voice, we can say, "I understand that you are mad and you want the teddy bear right away. Mommy is going to help you get it, but you have to come here with me. I'll lift you up and you can get it if you reach for it." With verbal children, we do the same thing while we talk to them. We have long discussions that combine words and gestures together.

The same type of process can be used with older children and adults with a variety of mental health problems, because these usually involve problems regulating emotions such as depression, fear, or anxiety, or regulating impulses in terms of conduct disorders and conduct problems. For example, with a narcissistic adult who doesn't experience closeness or dependency, who just kind of fakes it, the therapist needs to acknowledge—with gestures as well as words—the first signs of real warmth the person shows. After that, the therapist can help the person describe the feeling with words, and understand why it wasn't there originally and why the person had to fake it all these years.

The goal is to develop a continuous flow of back-and-forth communication through long conversations with gestures. Once the person develops the capacity for long, nonverbal interactions, he can learn to balance his emotions and make progress toward more regulated behavior. If the capacity is already there, but is just limited in terms of emotional range, then we work to broaden that range. Thus, developing the capacity for nonverbal interactions is the cornerstone for establishing a broad sense of self and others, and therefore for mental health overall.

Points to Remember

- Non-verbal communication, such as head nods, smiles, smirks, tone of voice, hand motions, body posture, raising of the eyebrows, and so forth, has specific importance to how we work with children and adults with mental and emotional challenges.
- It's easier to trust the non-verbal system of communication than the verbal system.
- Through predictable back-and-forth communication with the outside world (a smile begets a smile; a sound begets a sound) an infant develops the beginning of causal thinking and a sense of how reality works.
- By establishing a boundary between what is inside the infant and what is outside the infant; the sense of self and will is begins to form.
- The development or strengthening of engaged non-verbal communication is the foundation for mental and emotional health.
- The goal is to help the person first to express his or her emotions, and then to modulate and regulate these emotions.
- Whatever the person's age, empathetic non-verbal engagement should be the foundation of our interactions.

Chapter 5

Anxiety Disorders

Before addressing how to help people overcome anxiety disorders—or even, in many cases, to prevent the occurrence of these disorders in the first place—let's look at the developmental pathway that leads to anxiety. In terms of the DIR model discussed earlier, we believe that the biological contributions to this disorder express themselves through hyper-reactivity to different sensations—sounds, touch, surprising movements or other intense visual stimuli—and correspondingly strong emotional reactions, as well as an emotional reactivity to one's own feelings. In other words, internal feeling states tend to cause stronger reactions than they do in a typically developing person, whether these are physical sensations—a gurgle in the stomach or a fleeting discomfort in the head—or emotions. There tends to be a general reactivity to sensation and emotion and physiological background activity in the body.

These patterns occur very early in life. Newborn babies can be finicky and colicky, but when this sensitivity persists beyond the four- to six-month stage, it tends to take on the specific forms described above. Hyper-sensitivity can be a great asset in life: a reactive person can be very intuitive and can use this sensitivity to understand himself, others, and the world; this ability is key to becoming a skilled therapist, writer, or artist. But hyper-reactivity can be overwhelming, too; a child who has this pattern going into preschool, who is subjected to all the noise and commotion of the other children, can get overloaded easily and become frantic and anxious.

What kind of environment might help such an infant or child negotiate each of the early developmental stages (i.e., calm attention and engagement, exchanging emotional signals, shared problem-solving, and so forth)? If the child's caregivers are also hyper-reactive—if the child begins to get upset because he can't reach a toy he wants and Daddy responds anxiously, saying either, "We better get it for you quickly!" as though the roof were going to cave in, or, sternly, "No way am I going to help you!"—this will of course heighten the child's anxiety and reactivity.

On the other hand, if Daddy is very soothing and builds a back-and-forth conversation and counter-regulates as the child becomes anxious and fretful—saying something like, "Oh, we can get this together! Look, it's not so far! You want Daddy to help?" while nodding reassuringly, then the child might nod back. Then Daddy offers his hand; the child takes it; Daddy offers to pick him up; the child agrees and jumps into his arms; and together they can get the toy from the shelf. There might be few impatient whimpers or annoyed looks, but through this process of many gentle, pleasant interactions, the child is comforted and can achieve his objective. He begins to learn that he doesn't have to be controlled by his feeling state.

This kind of situation happens many times every day, at home and at school or daycare, with parents and with other caregivers. If the child experiences the first pattern, that his own anxiety causes anxiety in others, what lesson does he learn about himself and his nervous system? That the slightest little frustration leads to a volcano erupting. Whereas if he experiences the second pattern, that his anxiety leads to counter-regulating from others, he learns that he can overcome frustration, neediness, discomfort, and anxiety by interacting with others and working out a solution.

Now let's move forward into the next stage, when ideas, creative thinking, and connecting ideas together become important. The child (let's call him Tommy) might be a little more scared of the assertive or aggressive areas of life because he is very sensitive and hyper-reactive. He may be more prone to having nightmares or being afraid of the dark or, when he gets into the stage of connecting ideas together, of kidnappers coming and taking him away. The most helpful caregiving pattern for this child is soothing and regulating, involving many different emotional interactions, and also (gently) challenging Tommy in his pretend play to be more assertive. For example, Mommy's toy car blocks Tommy's car, so Tommy needs to figure out a solution in order to get where he wants to go, such as having his car grow wings to fly over Mommy's car.

Or, for example, we might have a little girl, Zoe, who likes everything to be very ordered or she gets anxious. While having a pretend tea party with Zoe, her grandmother might playfully take the part of an unruly guest who won't follow rules, so that Zoe gradually has to contend in a fun, imaginative way with dealing with conflict. Such challenges should be introduced very, very gradually, through lots of soothing interactions, fostering a sense of mastery and exploration, and broadening the range of feelings the child can embrace, even before creative ideas are used, at the stage of problem-solving with gestures. The key is to move slowly, step-by-step, allowing the child to master each step (that is, to be successful 70 to 80 percent of the time) before a new step is added on.

We can use this same process with preverbal, verbal, and creative experiences, and then when the child begins making logical sense of the world. At the higher levels of thinking, this process helps the child move from polarized thinking to gray-area thinking. He learns to see the subtleties and nuances of scary or mastery-oriented feelings with which he has a harder time, such as assertiveness. Peer play is encouraged with a gradually widening range of peers, so the child can get used to more rough-and-tumble-type kids, as well as to sweet, gentle children. When the child gets to the level of reflective thinking, at ages 10 to 14, he learns to understand himself as an individual with a sensitive nervous system that has both advantages and challenges, such as making certain feelings a little scarier, but one with which he has learned to be comfortable.

However, if this relationship pattern is not part of the environment, if there is a continuation of the hyper-reactivity on the caregiving side, pretend play is limited to themes of superficial compliance. Zoe has a nice little tea party, or Tommy just does his own thing with his cars and Mommy goes along with it, without broadening the creativity into realms that the child might find a little more challenging. We never get to reflective thinking and the child stays very polarized—all-or-nothing—in his thinking, and never advances to looking at subtleties or nuances because there's no experience of that in the family. He never learns to master challenging feelings through years of interactions with caregivers.

So here we see two pathways from the original physiological tendency to over-sensitivity. One leads to greater and greater anxiety and possibly the development of phobias as the child gets older. The other leads to more confidence, competence, and the ability to be assertive, as well as creativity, sensitivity, and empathy. Using our image of the inner security blanket, this is the difference between the warm comforting blanket and the one with the holes in it.

This latter pathway is simple to describe, but not simple to do in the context of hundreds or even thousands of interactions a day. What are the principles of working in a caregiving capacity with individuals (of any age) to help them master anxiety? Following the developmental stages, we first want to be soothing and regulating and always counter-regulating. Then, as we develop back-and-forth emotional signaling, we also encourage a sense of mastery and assertiveness, a "can-do" attitude, very gradually, with a 70 to 80 percent success rate for the person before moving on to the next stage.

We want to keep doing this as we help him think creatively, whether we're involved in pretend play with a child, writing stories with teenagers, or just imagining different scenarios with a colleague or spouse. We want to do this as we help the person make sense of things and have logical discussions. We want to put a lot of emphasis on looking at subtleties and gray-area thinking, particularly in the areas of assertiveness and mastery and coping with aggression. We want to do this as we encourage reflective thinking (self-understanding) in the person by asking questions about how he feels, how that compares to how he felt at other times or how other people feel, and so forth. As we soothe, counter-regulate, and encourage mastery and assertiveness at all these levels by breaking bigger steps down into small steps, we're creating an environment that helps the person overcome anxiety.

This general relationship environment can be coupled with special exercises such as relaxation exercises or other comforting activities like meditation, yoga, listening to music, and so forth for the older child or adult who already has fixed patterns. These activities can be employed to create a physiologic state of calm in the person while we facilitate the types of interactions described above.

Principles for Overcoming Anxiety

The principles for helping individuals overcome anxiety are the same as those that promote healthy development and help children and adults to not become anxious in the first place. Once anxiety is already present, then these principles have to be employed to an even greater degree. The first principle is to recognize the individual's biological differences; in the case of anxiety, these differences are often expressed in over-reactivity to sensation. So, anxious individuals may be very reactive to touch and sound and other sensations, as well as to their own emotions.

The second principle is to always try to counter-balance or counter-regulate in relationships, which means that as the individual gets anxious, we try to avoid becoming anxious ourselves, or becoming strident or reactive. Instead, we try to be extra soothing and regulating. The more anxious and frantic the person becomes, the more regulating, calming, and soothing we become.

Third, we help the individual put his anxieties, worries, and fears into words—with children, through pretend play, and with adults, through long, empathetic conversations. Talking about his fears won't make him worry more; the idea is to help the person elaborate and to go for depth rather than repetition. Often, the person may repeat his fears and worries, and doing that can be helpful up to a point, but then we have to help him go beyond repetition into telling us more about the nature of the fear, what it feels like in his body, what it reminds him of in terms of his own history. With children, we can help them draw it with crayons or play it out or put it into a drama if they can't discuss in great depth. In fact, with a child we don't have to even ask the question; it comes out naturally in the drama. With an adult, it can start with an explicit conversation, as long as the conversation is free, open, and unstructured as we don't want to interrogate the person.

The fourth principle is to help the person overcome his anxiety or find realistic solutions to challenges such as a job change or a family transition, that is, brainstorming in a practical, reality-based way. This step can also involve self-calming techniques, such as deep breathing, yoga, and various types of deep relaxation. With children, it's very important to get them physically active and confident in their own bodies. This is particularly true for children with anxieties, not just those who are over-reactive to sensation, as often they are less confident in the way their motor system works or the level of their coordination. So the idea here is to have a profile of a person's physical differences in terms of the way she expresses language, the way she processes sights, the way she deals with actions and with her body and see where she needs strengthening. Then we help her to be physically active and get plenty of enjoyable exercise through fun activities such as sports, dance, skating, swimming, and so forth. Those kinds of activities not only promote a healthy outlook, but also help to calm the nervous system.

Working With Anxiety—Case Study #1

Let's look at how these principles were used to help a young woman who grew up with a mother who was very reactive to her and very overprotective. This woman, Valerie, was very reactive as a child to touch and sound and also to smells and taste, and was still reactive when she came to therapy as an adult. Valerie was extraordinarily bright; she was valedictorian of her high school class and went on to an elite college. However, when, as a child, Valerie was fearful about new experiences, her mother would be very reactive in response. It was almost as if Valerie's fears made her mother scared.

The mother was an athletic and competent woman, and she seemed to be worried that Valerie wouldn't turn out like her. She was very quick to say things like, "Well, we can't run away from what scares us!" when Valerie was anxious about a new toy, a new acquaintance, or a new experience. Rather than gradually helping her daughter to experiment by saying things like, "Oh, my little baby—does the loud noise of the vacuum scare you? Well, what can we do? Can we move it over here?" she was very quick and to the point about wanting Valerie to get over her fears. Watching a videotape of them interacting when Valerie was a toddler, we could see that her mother's response time was very quick and abrupt, somewhat intrusive, and, rather than being counter-balancing, was accentuating Valerie's anxiety. So, often, as Valerie's anxiety mounted, her mother's motor movements would get more frantic, and her face would tighten up and she would get anxious, as if she were a toddler herself.

Needless to say, as a preschooler Valerie developed lots of fears about kidnappers and about disasters happening to her family, particularly her mother (which is not surprising, since a lot of anger had built up towards her mother). While she did very well in school, she was always scared that other children wouldn't like her, that people would reject her, and that she would fail; she lived under a cloud of anxiety all through her teenage years and into college. In college her anxiety about doing badly actually interfered with her creativity and innovation, so she was a B student, although she was easily capable of being an A student; her fear of "getting the wrong answer" stifled her expression.

Early in her marriage, Valerie also operated out of fear, the fear of displeasing her husband and her children. She was often agitated and finally came for therapy when her anxieties began interfering with her part-time work. She would sit at meetings and literally could not speak up to present her ideas because she was so fearful of making a mistake or having other people laugh at her or talk about her.

In therapy, we instituted the approach outlined above. Her therapist was always careful to be counter-regulating and soothing, while at the same time helping Valerie elaborate the nature of her fears and getting her involved in positive strategies for coping, such as relaxation and physical activity. While Valerie's thinking was very abstract and reflective in most areas, when she was anxious she had a polarized, "all-or-nothing" perspective and expected bad things to happen to her. Her therapist helped her to reason things out and look at shades of gray through understanding her feelings more. For example, if Valerie was nervous about a work project, he'd ask her to compare how scared she was about this project to how scared she was about the last project she did, and so forth.

Once the therapeutic relationship was well-established, the therapist asked permission for the family to come in, beginning with Valerie's husband. The therapist did some couples work to help the husband, who was himself reactive, just like Valerie's mother; he heightened Valerie's fears and anxieties. So the therapist outlined the principles above for the husband, and taught him to be calming and soothing and counter-regulating when his wife was anxious, and also to help his wife to counter-regulate when he himself was anxious. Then they practiced the techniques in their couples' sessions. If Valerie and her husband talked with each other about a problem, perhaps with one of their children, the therapist would point out where they were heightening each other's anxieties rather than counter-regulating and soothing. Instead of launching into practical advice, which was their tendency, they learned to listen and empathize and help each other elaborate and move into gray-area thinking.

The therapist helped them both to become a little more reflective and consider their own feelings and assess how they were doing. Once the husband got the hang of it, he came in once a month for follow-up sessions, and Valerie continued therapy once a week. Over the course of a year, Valerie made very good progress with this approach, which combined features of many therapeutic systems, including psychodynamic and cognitive behavioral therapies, under the broader umbrella of a developmental perspective. Here we are guided by developmental principles (i.e., understanding what causes anxiety in the first place) and then do what is helpful to the individual without limiting ourselves to a particular school of thought.

Working With Anxiety—Case Study #2

We took a similar approach with a little boy, Nathan, who at age four-and-a-half was having lots of separation anxiety from Mommy and was fearful of playing with other boys (who were "too rough"), preferring to play with girls instead. He was very fearful of "bad things happening to Mommy and Daddy" and would play out scenes of accidents and hurricanes in his pretend play. Nathan's mother worked full-time and Nathan's father worked half-time, so Nathan spent more time with his father. However, his father was very anxious and reactive, like the mother in the first case study. He was very competitive and had little patience for his passive son, who preferred to be a "couch potato." Every time Nathan was scared, his father would try to rouse him into physical activity; he'd become very abrupt and the tension would mount in his face as soon as his little guy showed vulnerability.

In therapy, the father revealed that he was very scared of his own vulnerabilities and embarrassed about not being the main breadwinner in the family; he and his wife were both attorneys, but she was more successful. As Nathan became a verbal preschooler, his father couldn't help him address the areas of vulnerability and competitiveness and competency in pretend play. They played out superficial dramas about dinner parties or about trucks delivering rocks or food to the school and the home, but there was nothing about conflict or about "good guys vs. bad guys" or saving fairy princesses. Every time Nathan would introduce such a theme that he picked up from a TV show or a movie, his father would quickly change the subject or dominate Nathan by being an opponent who had to win. He never let Nathan be the good guy who defeated the bad guy.

The approach we took was to help the father understand the nature of his conflicts around vulnerability. We taught him to counter-regulate, so that instead of being competitive, intrusive, and abrupt with his son, he could be soothing when Nathan was scared, while gradually encouraging Nathan's sense of assertiveness and mastery. We began with little things, like who would get the toy or who would reach into the refrigerator for the juice. Nathan, in addition to his sensory reactivity, had some clumsiness or what we call motor planning problems, so we incorporated lots of movement-oriented games that dealt with assertiveness and conflict. For example, he would have to chase and catch his father, or would have to climb over a balance beam to get to the bad guy and capture him and put him in the dungeon, or he could throw Nerf balls at Daddy to defeat the bad guy. These activities gave him more confidence in his body. So, through pretend play, the father helped Nathan elaborate the competitive side of life; the rule was that the little boy initially needed to win 70-80 percent of the time in the activities, whether it was an athletic game or a pretend play drama. Then we gradually moved it to 50 percent, so Daddy and Nathan could each win half of the time.

We also got Nathan's mother more involved by getting her home a little bit earlier to do some Floortime play with her son—that is, unstructured play time where the caregiver follows the child's lead. As Nathan became capable of answering "why" questions and being more logical, we encouraged both parents to have problem-solving discussions with Nathan to help him talk about his feelings—what scared him, what made him happy, what made him sad—and to be good listeners. After listening, empathizing, and helping Nathan elaborate his feelings about the problem, they could brainstorm with him to decide what they could all do about it.

This also involved, when the problem related to another child at camp or at school, helping Nathan to improve his reflective thinking by figuring out what the other child felt and why the other child was doing what he did. For example, one rough-and-tumble boy at school would always take Nathan's toys. The father first suggested that Nathan fight the other boy, but this scared Nathan. He said, realistically, "He's bigger and stronger than me. If I fight with him about it he will beat me up, so doing what Daddy says won't work." He also explained that telling the teacher or the other boy's parents wouldn't work because, "everyone will tease me for being a tattle tale."

In trying to figure out why the other little boy was taking Nathan's toys, the family realized that he came from a much less wealthy background and didn't have many toys at home. So, they came up with the strategy wherein Nathan would offer to share certain toys with the other boy, and even loan him certain toys to take home. He would do it actively and proactively, rather than reactively and grudgingly, and see if they could work out a classroom relationship. By reaching out to this child in a positive way and not acting intimidated or fearful, but inviting him to play with his toys and even letting him borrow some of them and letting him try others, Nathan actually developed a nice friendship with the other boy. The key to Nathan's growth was in taking action to solve a dilemma with no easy answer.

Through the family's work in therapy, the parents became more counter-regulating, so that Nathan was soothed when he became anxious, and could develop more assertiveness, imagination, and logical thinking to cope with his biological tendency toward anxiety. Nathan became more comfortable with assertiveness and mastery, more comfortable with his feelings, stronger in his coordination, and more confident in his physical self, in terms of both stamina and his ability to master his body. In the ten years since the original work, we've checked in with Nathan once a year as part of routine follow-up and he's thrived. He's successful at school and has lots of friendships. He's more on the cautious side than on the bold, daredevil side, but in a reasonably healthy and thoughtful way he tries new things and he feels good about himself. Nathan's inner security blanket is holding strong and growing along with him.

Points to Remember

To help prevent a person from becoming anxious, and to soothe and help the person overcome anxiety if it does occur, we want to:

- Take into account the person's biological tendencies and sensitivities
- Soothe and counter-regulate, through our words, our gestures and vocal tone, and through activities that are physically regulating
- Encourage a sense of mastery and assertiveness through pretend play (as appropriate) and the creative, symbolic expression of feelings
- Explore solutions that the person can employ on their own, such as self-calming techniques, and in relationship, such as brainstorming about a problem.

Chapter 6

Overcoming Depression

Depression is similar to anxiety, but with some important differences. On the physical side, the similarity is that individuals prone to depression tend to be hyper-reactive or hyper-sensitive to sensation—to touch, sounds, smells, and/or sights—and to their emotions; that's one of the reasons they have mood swings. Often they're sensitive to movement in space, so a child getting an "airplane ride" from Daddy may be a little scared and not enjoy it as much as another child might. When this sensitivity is coupled to sensation, there's often a tendency to have stronger verbal skills than visual-spatial skills. Individuals prone to depression may have a very good visual memory for details (i.e., the "trees"), but they may not be able to see the big picture ("the forest"), so they get lost in how they feel in the moment as opposed to seeing their situation in a larger context. Or, they may have strong visual-spatial skills that they actually use to support their depressive tendencies.

The Roots of Depression

In addition to these constitutional tendencies, which may be in some way genetic or result from prenatal influences that express themselves in the maturation of the nervous system, there also tend to be certain experiences that appear in the backgrounds of those with depression. Here the caregiving pattern tends to be very different from the one we see for anxiety. Whereas with anxiety the caregivers tend to be reactive and intrusive and not counter-regulating, with depression caregivers tend to freeze a little bit at moments of heightened affect or emotion. So the child raises an issue of conflict or gets annoyed or looks a little sad or despondent for a bit, and the caregiver, instead of wooing the child back into a sense of relating, tends to freeze.

When we watch family videotapes of children with depression, we see that their caregivers freeze a little bit and get quiet when the child is upset—they almost pull away at the moment of crisis. It may just be for a split-second or two, but at that moment the child experiences a loss of nurturing support—a loss of the available, loving caregiver—and instead feels an emptiness. Imagine that, as an adult, you're talking to a spouse or friend or family member. You hit a moment of heightened emotion, you're confessing an angry feeling or a sad feeling or an embarrassing feeling, and instead of seeing a nice, warm nod and an understanding look in the other person's eyes, and maybe a hearing an empathetic comment that helps you elaborate—the person just looks at you with a frozen expression. You might feel embarrassed, you might feel humiliated; at the deepest level you feel a sense of loss. This is what the infant or child experiences. (And the hypothetical thread holding that inner security blanket together starts to fray.)

What we've hypothesized is that the momentary lapse in responsiveness—that experience of loss—creates an inner sense of emptiness; the child can't use the emotion of the other person, the caregiver, in a reassuring way to fill himself up. A moment later, the caregiver may regroup and say the perfectly appropriate thing and may be empathetic, but often the pattern of disconnect continues, not so much with silence but with a difficulty resonating with the child's mood. The caregiver may attempt either to change the topic to something more positive or just move on to something else to distract the child. If there is an attempt to resonate with the child's mood, it's done to such a degree that it's much more intense than the child was conveying to begin with. So, as the interaction progresses, the caregiver doesn't offer a level of empathy that resonates with the child's experience. Also, the child doesn't experience that sense of sharing of an emotion with a loving, caring, trusted adult, which is so reassuring and comforting and which would enable him to regroup.

Repeated experiences like this set the stage, at the pre-verbal level, for the child to experience a dysphoric (non-positive, non-self-esteem-building, non-comforting) emotion. So, the child's physical tendencies, coupled with this dysphoric emotion, can create the basis for an early sense of aloneness, emptiness, or loss, and the feeling of a lack of support. When we speak to depressed individuals later on, this is often what they describe in the core of their gut.

As children with this combination of factors move into the verbal stage—into pretend play and the use of ideas—they have difficulty elaborating themes of security and of an internal positive image of a nurturing figure. In ordinary, healthy development, children can create in their own minds an internal feeling tone, based on the caregiving adult in their lives, which they can use for security at times of strong emotion. In other words, they carry their security blankets inside themselves. But in cases of depression, individuals don't have that internal security blanket, and so when pretend play themes have to do with frustration, loss, or disappointment, they tend to be either a bit overly aggressive in their play or else withdraw and express a little sadness or disappointment. Often the caregiver pattern of freezing at moments of strong emotion has continued, so the caregiver's response doesn't compensate for the child's experience at this stage, either.

This dynamic then continues through each of the developmental stages described earlier. The picture that emerges is of an individual who is hyper-reactive to sensation, who tends to be more detail-oriented than big-picture oriented in his thinking, and because she didn't have early experiences that counter-balanced her biological tendencies, she tends to feel abandoned and alone, with an inner sense of emptiness. She can't use ideas to verbalize her sense of emptiness or sadness; instead it's avoided, and at moments of strong emotion she is left with that inner feeling of emptiness. It's not surprising, then, that at a moment of crisis or stress—whether moving homes or schools, going off to college, starting a new job, ending a romantic relationship, or any number of other life challenges—at times when the person really needs that inner sense of security to fall back on, she doesn't have it. Instead, she has the experience of emptiness and aloneness, which leads to despondency and depression.

Often, coupled with this feeling of despondency or of being abandoned, there is lots of anger. Some individuals are more prone to feeling angry for other reasons as well, such as a tendency toward craving sensation in addition to being over-reactive to sensation. However, it could also be that when a person feels this inner sense of loss he gets very angry about it, and then turns his anger at himself and becomes very self-critical. Other individuals going through depression don't have the self-critical features; they just have the inner sense of emptiness, loss, and neediness, and tend to be a little more clingy and insecure.

Working with Depressed Individuals

When we look at what to do about this, again we look at what steps would have promoted positive mental health in the first place, and then we use those steps to help individuals overcome their depressive tendencies. It starts with recognizing the physical makeup of the toddler, child, or adult, which is being over-reactive to sensation and often being better at detail-oriented thinking than big-picture thinking. If the person is an adult, or even an older, verbal child, we help him recognize that that's what his physical make-up is and that it has many assets, such as increasing his sensitivity.

Second, we counter-balance and counter-regulate. If we're working with a child, we help the caregivers figure out why they tend to freeze—why strong emotion in their child is so scary to them—so that they can learn to interact more empathetically. Often they have causal factors in their own background such as those feelings were scary to their parents and to their parents' parents before them. This may be the legacy of many generations. We try to get the caregivers more comfortable with these scary feelings so they can be more responsive, empathetic, and counter-regulating with their child.

Basically, the goal for caregivers, therapists, spouses, or whoever is working with the child or adult is to woo the individual at the moment of strong emotion to maintain a rhythm of back-and-forth interaction. We don't want to do this by expressing phony positive emotions, but with empathetic questions and comments: "Oh, what a sad look you have! What can Mommy do to make you feel better?" or, "Did something upset you to make you stop playing with your toy?" or, "Goodness, that song must have really affected you to make you cry like that; do you want to talk about it?" We say something in a soothing, empathetic tone of voice that generates and keeps a feeling of warmth in the interaction, so the individual has something to think about. Silence on the part of the parent, spouse, or therapist may not be helpful here; you don't have to guide the dialogue, but you want to respond with a warm, empathetic rhythm because that's what makes the individual feel connected to you.

The third principle is to help the adult or the verbal child elaborate the nature of his sadness, the nature of the feeling of aloneness, again, always with a counter-balancing response so he feels your empathy, warmth, and involvement. It may take years of this kind of interaction for the person to really trust the emotional responsiveness of caregivers or confidantes, to overcome the earlier experiences.

If there's lots of anger and self-criticism, we help the person to elaborate those feelings—the anger over being abandoned and how that played out in childhood and how it tends to be looked for in adult relationships, even when it may not be there. The depressed person tends to see rejection and abandonment even when the other person is just coughing or is distracted, but is far from being rejecting. We often see this in younger adults in dating relationships. They're always feeling rejected, when the other person may just be busy or is not yet as in love as the other, or has trust issues of his or her own. The anger needs to be explored at whatever level the child or adult can elaborate it, so the individual gets comfortable with analyzing it. Just by talking about it he's less likely to direct it toward himself.

The next key ingredient in helping a person to overcome depression is to encourage him to remember experiences with his primary caregiver that *were* positive and nurturing (as few and far between as these may have been) and see if once the disappointment, loss, and anger are explored, he can use these positive experiences to begin to create that internal security blanket. If he can't remember any experiences with his primary caregiver, maybe there were experiences with a grandparent or a teacher, or with someone who's come into his life more recently, which can give him some solace and help him create that inner sense of security. Then, as he's capable, the next step is to help him move from polarized thinking around his depression—because all depression involves a lot of polarized thinking—to looking at the subtleties and nuances of his various feelings, his sadness, disappointment, anger, and depression. For example, depression is very different from sadness or disappointment; it includes a sense of loss and emptiness and self-criticism. We want to help individuals verbalize (or, if it's a pre-verbal child, to play out) the full range of feelings.

It's also very important to help the person become a big picture thinker by asking questions such as, "Well, how does all that fit together? How does the behavior of this kid at school connect with the other kids you know? What's the bigger pattern here?" Maybe one kid is rejecting and mean but two others aren't; maybe the person has three difficult colleagues but one very pleasant one and two neutral ones. We help the person look at the whole framework—the "forest" instead of just the "trees," because when she's depressed she tends to see everything through the mood or through the lens of her feeling of the moment.

Treating Depression—A Case Study

Eight-year-old boy Tommy was getting more and more depressed. He avoided hanging out with his friends, he was spending more time playing computer games and watching TV, and he had a negative attitude about school and about his prospects for making friends. He basically felt that he was a failure, and at times he would even verbalize feelings such as, "I wish I were never born." He clearly looked and felt extremely sad. It was beyond just temporary sadness or disappointment about a particular situation with kids at school; it was at the point where he was retreating from his regular activities and just feeling depressed and like a failure.

Tommy fit our physiological profile for depressed individuals. He was very reactive to sensation—to both touch and sound—and was also very emotionally reactive to his own feelings and to those of others. He might interpret a faint grimace or a little smile on someone's face as a negative reaction to him or to something he did, as a sign that he was not as socially skillful as other children. He was a bright child and could verbalize many of his feelings. He also was very strong in terms of visual-spatial processing and had the ability to be a big-picture thinker. In the long term this could work for him, but in the short term it actually contributed to his depression because his tendency toward polarized thinking meant that he was very quick to construct big patterns, such as, "Nobody likes me." Rather than seeing shades of gray or seeing the glass as both half full and half empty, he would see it as all empty, using his long-term history to create a pattern around the feeling.

His strong big-picture thinking also meant that he dealt with his over-reactivity to sensation not by being fragmented or just cautious (as many sensory-reactive children can be), but by being stubborn and negative. He would anticipate that a situation or an experience would make him overloaded and then would just refuse to do it, whether it was wearing clothes that were the slightest bit rough, or going into a social situation such as a birthday party where he anticipated that people might make fun of him. He was very controlling about his environment, which is why he retreated to the safety of computer games and TV and "couch-potato land." We can see very clearly this combination, often, in both adults and children who get depressed. They combine their over-reactivity to sensation with a strong capacity for big-picture thinking. So rather than just getting fragmented in a stressful situation and jumping from thought to thought, they actually see a whole pattern that depresses them, and they become negative and stubborn, which just digs the hole deeper for them. However, in the long term they can learn to use this skill to dig themselves out of a depression, because they can get some insight into their feelings and patterns and take corrective action to change them.

Tommy's background also evidenced some of the characteristics discussed above. We learned by watching family videotapes that, as a small child, when he would get intense in his moods or very negative or very stubborn or looked depressed, his mother would freeze a little bit and blame herself for his mood. Rather than just trying to comfort and soothe Tommy and bring him out of his mood, she would momentarily sort of freeze; you could see in her face a build-up of tension. So he experienced during those moments of intense emotion an absence of any emotion coming back from the caregiver on whom he was most dependent. Instead he got an empty response or a tense response, which didn't "fill him up," as he later came to describe it. Indeed, by the time he came to therapy, whenever he felt strong emotions they were coupled with pessimism and an empty feeling, which dated back, in all likelihood, to these pre-verbal experiences with his mother.

The same patterns repeated themselves in Tommy's pretend play. If it were just a nice little scenario about trucks or stuffed animals going to school, his mother played out imaginative pretend dramas with him. But when themes of aggression, conflict, or other intense emotions arose, his mother got worried, and wondered, "Why are these in his play? What does this mean? Am I a bad mother?" And she would freeze again and Tommy would experience that same lack of empathy and his experience of emptiness would be reinforced. When we worked with him in therapy, he described when he felt strong negative feelings—anger or sadness or rejection—he couldn't picture feeling better. He had no images or words in his mind that he could draw on to make himself feel better or to reassure himself.

Many of us go through tough times, but at the moment of crisis we can reassure ourselves and talk ourselves out of it, or we picture something positive to help us get through it. This ability derives from experiences we had while growing up in which if we were distressed or upset or sad, there was somebody holding our hand, empathizing, giving us hope or promises of a better future. But Tommy didn't have that, so at the level of pre-verbal or pre-symbolic experience there was a sense of emptiness at the moment of intense emotion. Then, at the stage of using images or symbols with words or pictures, that emptiness was reinforced rather than ameliorated; he couldn't form symbols to express it and move beyond his depression.

As Tommy began moving into causal and logical thinking, he had unrealistic expectations—in the sense of the reality of the situation at hand—for continuing empty or negative or bad experiences. These expectations, coupled with strong affect, made him more vulnerable to depression. It was also hard for him to progress into gray-area thinking and higher forms of reflective thinking around intense feelings, although he was quite able to do this with unimportant topics and with his schoolwork. Tommy was a strong student, although when he got very depressed his grades started suffering because he stopped doing his homework and handing in assignments.

In addition to the dynamic with Tommy's mother, the dynamic with his father was problematic as well. Tommy's father was a busy attorney who got home late at night and didn't have much patience. When Tommy got negative or stubborn, Dad would take an inflexible, militaristic attitude; his response to Tommy's mood was often, "Okay, let's get over it; let's tough it out." He thought he could intimidate Tommy into "toeing the line" and doing whatever it was he was supposed to do, whether it was wearing proper clothing or sitting at the dinner table. Tommy's father played with him occasionally, but when he did, it was generally either roughhousing or trying to teach Tommy to play sports. It wasn't empathetic, flexible play that focused on Tommy's interests. Over time, Tommy began to avoid playing with his father because of his controlling, brusque style, even though Tommy enjoyed sports and wanted to be active. The tension and conflict in their relationship intensified.

So we had a situation with a mother who was more "there" and more empathetic, but who couldn't handle Tommy's intense emotion, causing him to experience a feeling of emptiness, and a father who was oriented toward power struggles with his negative and stubborn little boy. When Tommy's depression reached a peak, the family came in for a consultation and we identified these patterns. We also identified the principles that could help overcome his depression. As a result, we instituted the following plan to help Tommy master some of the developmental stages that he had not yet mastered, as this lack of mastery was making him vulnerable to depression.

First, we helped Tommy's mother understand her own background and her relationship with her own mother, who had been very rigid and intrusive and who hadn't handled intense emotion well. These insights enabled her to hang in there with Tommy when he showed strong emotion. She began to be more flexible and empathetic and to listen to Tommy's anger or conflict or pain without blaming herself. When she felt the urge to blame herself, she was able to talk herself through it, "I know I feel this way because of what I experienced with my own mom, but I don't need to repeat the pattern. I'm going to hang in there and provide a different experience for my little guy." Gradually Tommy began experiencing his mother not as an empty space at critical moments, but as an empathetic presence. That was a very important development; despite his age, it's never too late to achieve that internal security blanket, that empathetic image or relationship you can carry around inside.

Next, we worked with Tommy's father to change his own patterns. Once Tommy began verbalizing feelings of wishing he had never been born, it got his father's attention and he realized that his rough, rigid style wasn't working with his son, even though this was his idea of how parents should get their little boys to be tough and rugged. He recognized, with the help of the therapist, that the pathway to helping Tommy was through more warmth and empathy and through Floortime. So the father started getting home earlier in the evenings and doing one or two Floortime sessions with his son. They started off playing computer games and then board games that Tommy liked, and then they were actually able to go out in the back yard and dribble a basketball together. The father started teaching Tommy the athletic skills that Tommy wanted to learn. The key factor was that the father began interacting very flexibly, always setting up games in which Tommy could win 70 to 80 percent of the time. They began having a better time together, throwing balls around, playing Nerf baseball, and doing some fantasy play together, in which there was usually a theme of Tommy dominating his father, rather than the other way around, which had been the earlier theme.

With Dad getting home earlier, there was more general family time, too. Tommy had an older sister, and Tommy became less intrusive and provocative with her and, therefore, their relationship became more harmonious and the whole family started getting along better. In his therapy sessions, Tommy gradually became a little more flexible and his stubbornness and negative expectations were less intense. He still had his worries, such as about the kids at school being mean, but the worrying went from a 10-plus to a seven, and then eventually down to a five. Everything softened a little bit, although the patterns were still there.

We also instituted problem-solving time in which Tommy's parents helped him anticipate the next day, the good and the bad things that might happen, and the feelings he might have in response to whatever happened. We emphasized moving from polarized thinking to gray-area thinking. For example, they would ask, "How do you think tomorrow will be compared to today? Do you think the guys will tease you more or less? How will you feel—sad or angry? Will there be anything that goes well tomorrow?" Through this "Thinking About Tomorrow" game, over a period of many months Tommy moved more into gray-area thinking, and even began anticipating some positive things that would happen the next day. Tommy continued to be a big-picture thinker, but now that he was using this skill in anticipatory problem-solving he realized that he always anticipated the worst. Happily, when he came home the next day and talked about what happened at school, it wasn't as bad as he'd thought it would be. So now his big-picture thinking ability was an advantage in terms of self-generated insight.

Also, in the problem-solving, "Thinking About Tomorrow" discussions, Tommy talked about how the next day at school might be tough because there would be a lot of noise, and he didn't like noisy environments, or because there was going to be an assembly, which meant that the kids couldn't wear sweatpants and he wasn't looking forward to having to wear chinos, which made him uncomfortable. Through these discussions, Tommy became more aware of how his body was more sensitive than other people's might be, and how that made him feel. He talked about his reaction to his own sensory experiences, including how sensitive he was both to touch and to different kinds of sound, as well as how quickly he picked up on how other people looked at him and talked to him—their tone of voice.

Tommy's father gave him lots of examples of how, as a child, he had been similar to Tommy, and how he then overcompensated in the other direction as a teenager. He explained that Tommy could use his sensitivity to his advantage to size up people and understand their feelings. Then the family began broadening the problem-solving discussions to include not only how Tommy thought he would feel the next day, but also how he thought the other people he was interacting with—other students, or his teachers, for example—would feel in the particular situation he was anticipating. Understanding how his physical make-up worked and how it influenced his feelings gave Tommy additional tools to begin overcoming not just his immediate depression, but also his overall tendencies toward depression. Now that he had a stronger internal sense of security, he was a better gray-area thinker, and he understood that he was a sensitive person who could feel things deeply and intensely, and that capacity could be an advantage as well as a disadvantage.

Finally, Tommy's father agreed to coach the local recreation department soccer team, on which Tommy played, and that enabled Tommy to feel more secure socially, particularly now that he had a better relationship with his dad. Because he was practicing a lot with his father in the backyard, Tommy was actually a pretty good soccer player, so instead of being scape-goated by his friends, there was now a more reciprocal and mutual pattern, with some teasing back and forth. Tommy no longer felt like the neighborhood loser.

Tommy is now an adult, but he can remember his childhood years of being negative and depressed. He is still in touch with those feelings of insecurity and rejection, but he uses them for insight into his work as a teacher. He has a particular knack for working with kids who are sensitive and need that little extra warmth and empathy. Because he's a good big-picture thinker, he's also very effective at figuring out innovative ways to get across to the kids.

The important principles to remember when working with individuals with depression are, first, to recognize and help them understand their unique physical make-up, their sensitivity to sensation and therefore to affect. Second, often these individuals had at a formative stage experiences with caregivers that left them without an internal sense of security. It's important, if working with a child, to change that in the family pattern, and if you're working with an adult, to create experiences that build that sense of security. The third principle is to help the individual experience flexibility and empathy rather than power struggles, and move from polarized thinking to gray-area thinking. Finally, we want to help the individual develop a more assertive attitude towards life, and cope with the competition and anger that goes along with it, instead of retreating into self-defeating attitudes. As with the case study of Tommy, we've seen these principles play out successfully for many children and adults as a comprehensive intervention for depression.

Points to Remember

A comprehensive intervention to prevent or overcome depression includes the following principles:

- Recognize and help the person understand their unique physical make-up, their sensitivity to sensation and therefore to affect.
- Address the impact of the early experiences with caregivers that left the individual without an internal sense of security: when working with a child, help to change the dynamic in the family pattern; if you're working with an adult, create experiences that build that sense of security.
- Help the individual experience flexibility and empathy rather than power struggles, and move from polarized thinking to gray-area thinking.
- Help the individual develop a more assertive attitude towards life, and cope with the competition and anger that goes along with it, instead of retreating into self-defeating attitudes.

Chapter 7

Attentional Problems, Including ADD and ADHD

Attentional problems, including ADHD and ADD, are frequently seen in children with special needs, but are also seen in children who are gifted learners and in children who have one or more of a variety of learning challenges—almost everyone potentially can have some attentional challenges. Some of them reach the threshold where they are diagnosed with ADD or ADHD; that diagnosis is being made much more widely these days and is often treated only with medication. We hope to show in this chapter that medication is a limited approach and should be considered, if at all, only as part of a comprehensive treatment program.

It has been estimated that as many as 10% of children have sufficient symptoms of attentional disorders to be diagnosed with ADD or ADHD. Many others are just beneath that threshold. So we are talking about a huge number of our population. The most common symptoms are distractibility, hyperactivity, inability to sustain attention and focus, inability to carry out complex multi-step directions, and complaints from the children themselves that it is hard for them to follow through or sit still or pay attention. Some children are very active and are always moving around and fidgeting. Others become self-absorbed and seem to get lost in daydreams. Still others simply get distracted. As one child told me in a lovely way, "Oh, I just pondered the tree outside—it was much more interesting than listening to my teacher. But I wish I could listen to my teacher because then I would know what the homework was because I didn't know what to do and didn't do very well on the test the next day."

ADD and ADHD affect not just children but adults as well. Many individuals are not diagnosed with ADD or ADHD until they are in their 20s or 30s and have difficulties at work or in graduate school or in their marriages, or with their own children. They are often treated the same way children are, with the same medications. So this is an adult's disorder as much as it is a child's disorder. Its origins are thought to begin in childhood but sometimes not until life becomes more complex and demanding is the problem or challenge evident. It is important to see this as a lifespan challenge; with each stage of development and at each age there may be different ramifications, manifesting in one's academic life, marriage, job, family life, and so forth.

What is the nature of ADD/ADHD—or, more broadly, attentional problems—and the developmental pathways that lead to them? What we have discovered recently, although many occupational therapists have noted this for some time, is that there are many different pathways, and there are both physical and biological differences, as well as experiential differences, in each of these pathways.

The Common Profiles of Individuals with Attentional Challenges

Some children with symptoms of distractibility are hyper-reactive to basic sensations such as touch, sound, sight, smell, and taste, so they get distracted very easily. If their environment is characterized by lots of sensory experiences, they are constantly overloaded, overwhelmed, and fragmented and they never learn to pay attention. If this physical tendency is matched with an environment where the caregivers tend to be busy or anxious and not themselves gifted at long chains of back-and-forth communication (both pre-verbal and verbal), and the child's early experience is not characterized by longer and longer chains of these interactions with more and more complex problem-solving, the child doesn't master focusing and attending. So if the caregiver tunes in to the child only for a moment here and there, and the child is distracted by her own over-reactivity to sensation, then the distractibility gets more and more severe as the child gets older. As adults, people with this profile may be very talented but also "all over the place." The over-reactive child or adult needs a very soothing, organized environment, as well as interactions with long circles of communication that help keep them focused.

Another pathway to attentional disorders is the opposite pattern: under-reactivity to sensations. Sound, touch, or smell hardly register, so you have to really energize up to get the person's attention. This kind of person tends to get absorbed by her own inner life—her gas bubbles as a baby or her own fantasies by age three or four. As an adult, she can be absorbed by her own ruminations about life or philosophy or relationships. This individual requires a highly energizing environment—just the opposite of what the over-reactive person needs. However, the environment should be energized in an organized, not random, way, and soothing when necessary.

An under-reactive person needs to be drawn out with lots of consistent high energy, with the same goal of long conversations, many circles of communication starting at the preverbal level as an infant and toddler. Once children are school-age, we can continue to help them practice focusing and attending. We do this not by forcing them to pay attention, but by making ourselves or the conversation so interesting or compelling that the child wants to focus. I rarely see a child who won't stay focused when the subject is of great interest to her. If she loves ice skating, books, or computer games, and you talk about that—all of a sudden the child is focused, even if she gets distracted when you talk about schoolwork.

There is another type of pattern that we call sensory-seeking. This is a child who seeks out a lot of sensation, who seems to crave touch, sound, and movement. This kind of child is more vulnerable to having attentional problems as well as hyper-activity, or at least lots of rough-and-tumble play. This pattern requires an environment that is very organized and provides organized, socially meaningful forms of activity. You can keep a child like this focused, even as a toddler, by playing active games like horsey rides where the child directs you with pointing and vocalizations. The idea is to channel the child's need for activity into interactive, meaningful games. The child is a cowboy and you are the horse, the child is the captain of a ship, and you are the ship, or you are a dragon and the child is a knight chasing you around the park.

The important thing is that the activity includes back-and-forth communication, that you are opening and closing many circles of communication, first with preverbal signaling and then with verbal dialogue. Children with this tendency, if their need for activity is channeled appropriately, may grow into adults who are athletes, explorers, or fire fighters. But if the tendency is intensified because the child's urges are being stifled, or the child is allowed to run around all over the place with no limits, then the child's need for sensation can lead to problems like experimenting with drugs or other harmful behaviors as she grows older, in addition to attentional problems.

These are the three most common patterns, but there can be other ones. Some children can be over-reactive in one modality, such as sound, and under-reactive in another modality, such as touch, and be sensory seeking for movement, for example. When interacting with people who have mixed patterns, we have to be soothing in some ways, energized and compelling in other ways, and very attentive to how activity is organized. This may seem like a tall order, but the earlier you start tuning into your child and understand her unique profile, the easier it is. This both prevents the attentional problems from getting very severe and can also, more importantly, turns the child's profile into an asset. The child who craves sensation may become an athlete; the under-reactive child who gets lost in her own fantasies may become a novelist; the over-reactive, highly sensitive child may become a teacher or therapist because of her ability to tune in.

Creating Helpful Environments

We can turn any pattern into an asset by providing a healthy, corrective environment that helps the individual, no matter what her age, master attention and organization by strengthening the first six stages of development: regulation and interest in the world, engagement, back-and-forth circles of communication, shared problem-solving, and then the creative and logical use of ideas. As we tailor the environment, our interactions, and the person's experiences to her individual profile, we help her develop the capacities she needs to turn her unique physical makeup—her biological tendencies—into an asset rather than a liability.

Corrective experiences are soothing when the child is hyper-reactive, energized when the child is under-reactive, and harness the child's activity when she is sensory-seeking in an interactive, socially meaningful, focused manner, through activities like sports or ballet rather than just running around and roughhousing. These experiences should also help the person become better than average at each of the stages of development. For children, this means more availability from caregivers, more pretend play, and more imagination and fantasy because we want the child to use creativity to work with her physical tendencies. It means developing stronger logic and reflective thinking because we want the child to be self-evaluative, to be able to say, "Gee, I'm getting distracted by that sound outside, I better put in an extra effort to listen to the teacher." We want the adult to be able to say, "Uh oh, I'm getting absorbed in my own fantasies rather than listening to what my husband is saying," and so forth. We want the person to master all the stages of social and intellectual development, so that she can understand and work with her physical profile.

The Role of Anxiety and Insecurity in Attentional Challenges

Anxiety and insecurity intensify the person's biological pattern, and increase attentional challenges. When a person gets anxious, she gets tense, and then she tends to be more distractible; anxiety brings out a person's natural tendency, whether it is to be over-reactive, under-reactive and self-absorbed, or sensory seeking. So it is very important to help people with attentional identify what it is that makes them feel insecure or anxious.

For example, a little girl named Jessica was very anxious around writing because she had fine motor delays, which often accompany attentional challenges. Whenever she had a writing exercise, Jessica would get very anxious because she felt like "my body doesn't work," as she put it. She would have negative thoughts about herself and would distract herself (and others) by talking to the child next to her and becoming the class clown, which made her teachers complain about her. It's easy to imagine how anxiety and insecurity would make sensory-seeking children more active and maybe even aggressive at times because they feel so bad about themselves that they want to act out. The under-reactive child, on the other hand, can really pull away when anxious, and become very self-absorbed and lost in a fantasy world.

It is very important to help children (and adults) identify what is making them feel unsure of themselves and to verbalize their anxiety, so it's no longer something secret and shameful, because shame just intensifies anxiety. Then, we want to help them strengthen the capacity in which they are weak, for example, their fine motor skills.

Motor Planning and Sequencing

Motor planning and sequencing (technically known as "praxis") is the ability to carry out an intent requiring a complex set of actions or steps. For example, a toddler may lead her daddy to a shelf to reach for a toy she wants. Or an older child, having an idea ("Gee, I want to build a fort"), can then plan the steps of getting the equipment and supplies to build the fort. Motor planning and sequencing challenges are called dyspraxia, or apraxia.

In a survey of 100 children with attentional problems—whether they had under-reactive, over-reactive, or sensory-seeking profiles—we found that about 80% also had motor planning and sequencing challenges. Occupational therapists have observed this correlation for some time. We also found that when we helped children improve their motor planning and sequencing abilities, their attention improved as well. The best way to improve motor planning and sequencing is by having a child practice it through activities that she loves to do. So, we follow the child's lead in terms of activities, but we set up challenges that require more and more steps. If the child wants to be a bandit hiding out in a fort, we create an obstacle course that she has to negotiate to get to the fort. The child is highly motivated to think through the steps and get to the fort, and is strengthening praxis by having fun.

Sometimes the challenge is with fine motor abilities, such as copying letters and shapes, and sometimes it's more with gross motor abilities, such as sports skills or dance steps. But the more the child does the activity, the more the skill improves. This is true for adults, too. In addition, motor planning and sequencing improve as we strengthen each of the social, emotional, and intellectual milestones. For example, a teenager who is reflective can reflect not only on what her goals are, but on how close she is to achieving them. She can create a chart to keep herself on target, so she can look at it and say, "OK, there are eight steps to doing this science project. I am on step three right now, and I have to accomplish the rest of the steps by this weekend." She can hang the chart in a prominent place in her room because she knows that if it isn't visible, she may forget about it. So, she uses her reflective ability to improve her planning and sequencing abilities. In this way, strengthening the thinking capacities helps improve both focus and attention, and motor planning and sequencing challenges.

A Note about Medication

It's very popular to prescribe medication to children with attentional challenges such as ADD and ADHD. But we have found that only about one in every 10 children we see with attentional problems eventually requires medication; with the rest, strengthening the developmental building blocks is sufficient, and these children actually do better long term than children on medication do. When medication is needed, it should be in addition to strengthening the building blocks.

Examples of Working with Attentional Challenges

The Toddler with Attentional Challenges

Jason was 15 months old when his parents brought him to us because he simply ran from toy to toy and activity to activity, rather than being able to focus on any one thing. We observed that Jason's mother, while being very loving and sweet, was also very distracted. Although she could afford it, she didn't have enough help around the house, and was overwhelmed with distractions and with caring for Jason's siblings. Her tendency to be fragmented intensified Jason's pattern of being fragmented. Jason's father, although he was more focused, worked late and wasn't very available; he would get home just before Jason went to bed.

We addressed Jason's burgeoning attentional challenges by bringing in a helper to look after the other children, so Jason's mother could have long sequences of interaction with her son with no distractions. The goal was to get 50+ circles of communication in a row, whether it was around going outside, finding a toy, getting a snack, or whatever interested Jason. Mother learned to stretch interactions out by adding steps: "Oh do you want to go outside? Oops—the door is stuck! How do we open it? Who is going to help us?" and so forth.

We strengthened Jason's motor planning and sequencing, we strengthened his focus by keeping him motivated, and we incorporated a lot of games like hide-and-go-seek and treasure hunts with gestural, verbal, and visual clues to get all parts of his nervous system working together in a more organized way. When Jason got older and went to preschool, his pretend play reflected his increased coordination. At each stage of his development, we continued having lots of long, one-on-one conversations to strengthen his development.

Jason's father was able to support the program by coming home earlier and then doing some of his work after Jason went to sleep and on weekend mornings, giving him more family time. He also learned how to interact with his son in the same way that the mother did. The program worked out very well and Jason became very gifted at school and very organized. Both parents were amazed when Jason's first grade teacher said he was one of her more organized students.

The Adult with Attentional Challenges

At the other end of the spectrum, a 48-year-old man named Harry was very successful as a businessman, but became overloaded and fragmented when he took on a new business venture in addition to the two he already had going. Juggling three businesses made it hard for him to focus on any of them, and to respond to his wife and children, who were getting frustrated with him. Harry had always been very hyper-responsive (verging on over-reactive) to his environment; he was so creative and masterful that he could just throw out ideas to his helpers, and they would pick up the projects and carry them forward so Harry didn't get overloaded. However, Harry's key assistant, who had worked for him for many years, had recently retired, and Harry's attentional challenges became more evident as he tried to handle more responsibilities himself.

We discovered that if Harry paid more attention to his hyper-responsivity and planning and sequencing challenges, he could compensate for them with his considerable intelligence and reflective abilities. We also found that he had visual-spatial challenges, that he tended to focus on the details of the trees rather than seeing the whole forest. His insights into details had enabled him to be very successful in business and in life, but he realized that he had a poor sense of direction and often couldn't see the big picture. For example, when he watched a movie, he had trouble following a complex plot or understanding how everything fit together.

Just this awareness encouraged Harry to use his intelligence to become more of a big picture thinker. We also did some exercises with him to strengthen his visual-spatial thinking; for example, we played the "Thinking About Tomorrow" game, which works as well for adults as for children. In this game you anticipate what you will be doing the following day. You create a film of it in your mind and visualize the situations that might arise, how you routinely deal with them, what some alternatives are, how you are going to feel, what the other people you'll be interacting with will feel and do, and so forth. We also did what "architectural exercises"—building structures with blocks and then building mirror images of the structure from different perspectives.

It's important to note that many people with attentional challenges have visual-spatial processing challenges in addition to motor planning and sequencing difficulties. A wonderful little book, *Thinking Goes To School*, by Hans Furth and Harry Wachs, gives many helpful visual-spatial exercises for verbal children and for adults. Many of the same exercises also address motor planning and sequencing challenges.

Finally, Harry started psychotherapy to address his marital and family problems. In therapy, he was helped to identify the sources of his anxiety—getting older (his father had passed away at a young age), feeling his memory wasn't as sharp as it had been—and learned that he was compensating for this fear by trying to do more rather than staying focused and doing fewer things more effectively, both in his work and home life. Through this process, and through strengthening his big picture thinking, Harry started doing very well and overcame the problems caused by his attentional challenges.

Points to Remember

Attentional disorders may be accompanied by motor planning challenges, visual spatial challenges, and anxiety. No matter which pattern predominates, similar principles apply in terms of treatment–we want to strengthen the first six developmental levels–though the specifics will, of course, differ depending on the individual's unique processing profile.

- The over-reactive individual needs a soothing, organized environment, and long, sustained interactions to help them focus.
- The under-reactive person requires an environment that's energizing in an organized way, and should be drawn out of his or her isolation with high-energy, sustained interactions.
- The sensory-seeking person–who can tend toward hyperactivity–needs to have his or her energy directed in active, involving activities that build the person's ability for interactions with many circles of communication.
- A comprehensive intervention will in most cases eliminate the need for medication; if medication is prescribed, it should only be as part of an intervention that includes the techniques described above.

Chapter 8

Obsessive Compulsive Patterns

Who among us doesn't engage in certain ritualistic, repetitive thoughts or actions? It's like the old sidewalk game we all played as children: "Step on a crack; break your mother's back." It was a fun game, yet also magical thinking; we obsessively avoided the cracks in the sidewalk as we walked down it. As adults, we may automatically use phrases such as "knock on wood" to prevent something bad happening to us, or we may feel uncomfortable and anxious if our little daily routines have to change for some reason. We all have bits and pieces of obsessive behavior or repetitive thoughts that we often use to ward off danger or anxiety.

Children, when they are fearful or anxious, also repeat certain actions to reduce their anxiety. With children with special needs or autistic spectrum disorders, we call these repetitive behaviors "perseveration." Some children who engage in this kind of behavior are just repeating motor patterns that they have learned because they don't have the flexibility to do more innovative problem-solving actions. Others may be coping with anxiety or emerging fears even as thoughts or ideas are coming into their minds for the first time. And of course we have all seen professional baseball players, for example, who come to a critical at bat and then stop to button and rebutton their batting gloves, adjust their stance, etc. till their anxiety is under control.

Fears and anxieties also exist at a preverbal level—at a developmental stage before the use of ideas. For example, we see that 16-month-olds, who don't have very many words at all, can still be scared by a monster, or they may have feelings of fear or dread that are unconnected to an image of a specific scary thing such as a wolf or a tiger. Even as adults we have these fearful feelings with no images at all. We may say to our spouse or to a good friend, "I don't know—I'm not worried about anything specific; I just feel apprehensive today for no reason at all."

The Developmental Pathway to Obsessive Compulsive Disorder

What is the developmental pathway toward obsessive thoughts or behaviors? As with our considerations of anxiety, depression, and the other common mental health problems, obsessive compulsive patterns also have their own developmental pathway involving biological elements and experiential ones.

Let's begin by looking at the biological aspects. Sharing a certain similarity to the pathways to anxiety and depression, the pathway to obsessive compulsive patterns usual involves sensory hyper-reactivity, beginning in early infancy. In other words, individuals prone to this pattern tend as a group to be over-reactive to sensation. Sounds, touch, bright lights, or dramatic movements may overwhelm them easily during infancy and toddlerhood, and even into the preschool years. Sometimes this persists into the older child, adolescent, and adult years. This tendency often makes the individual more prone to anxiety because if the world is overwhelming all the time, it seems like a scary, dangerous place—a lion's roar in a TV cartoon that's meant to be funny can sound terrifying. The activity of lots of children playing at preschool, the noise and speed of a ball game in P.E. class, or hearing a friend or boss yell can be more frightening than would normally be the case, simply because of the sensory over-stimulation.

As we saw in the developmental pathway to anxiety, caregivers can have different responses to the over-reactive child. If they over-react to the child's over-reaction, then there is a double whammy of anxiety. Every time the child gets overwhelmed and starts looking fearful, the caregiver exclaims, "OH MY GOD! WHAT'S HAPPENING?! WHAT'S WRONG?!" and then the child is doubly alarmed. He might just have been a little bit alarmed, but then he sees alarm in the eyes of the other person and thinks, "Things must be really bad if Mommy looks so panicked."

On the other hand, if the caregiver is very soothing and yet very interactive, saying "What's the matter, Sweetheart? Has something got you scared? How can I help make it better?" then the child learns to engage in soothing, organizing, back-and-forth exchanges of emotional signals, or circles of communication. As we discussed in the chapter on the nonverbal system, through these kinds of exchanges, children learn to negotiate anxious feelings. They can communicate even before they use words if this exchange is continuous, flexible, and comforting, and learn to reach out to others to become soothed, and eventually to internalize that soothing feeling. That soothing feeling is, of course, the inner security blanket.

Then, as children become more verbal and get ideas and can create fantasies, they play these themes out in pretend play: the mommy doll will reassure the baby doll. Eventually, children learn to soothe themselves, and the four-year-old child can say to himself, "It's not so bad, I don't need to feel so scared." Many adults talk themselves down or through an anxious situation, saying "I'm sure she got home safely and she just forgot to call me. I won't worry about it tonight." Otherwise, they can let their fears run wild, "Oh my God, was she in an accident? Should I call the police?"

The question, however, is when this biological tendency exists toward over-reactivity, and the environment doesn't offer soothing experiences at the different developmental stages all the way through adulthood (i.e., the individual doesn't have soothing relationships with spouses or friends), why do some individuals become obsessive and compulsive while others become anxious? What is the determining factor?

What we have found in individuals prone to obsessive compulsive patterns is that, as a group, they tend to have stronger visual-spatial abilities, stronger big-picture thinking, and, along with that, a stronger need for control over their environment. In comparison, individuals just prone to anxiety and panic tend to be more focused on the details, the "trees," and therefore don't tend to try to control the world around them as much. Of course, these are the extremes. Many individuals are close to the middle, so it's not always easy to form these neat categories, but in general, individuals prone to obsessive compulsive patterns tend to want to control their environments because their skill in big picture thinking causes them to anticipate what is coming, and they don't want to get overwhelmed.

Their stubbornness, negativity, and obsessive thought patterns or ritualistic behavior are part of this attempt to exercise control over their environment. Thus, the goal in addressing these patterns is to help the person calm down and assert some measure of control over her environment so she doesn't get overloaded. Typically, for example, children with this pattern refuse to wear certain socks because they feel too rough and that overloads them, or they may refuse to go to school because it is too noisy. Adults with obsessive compulsive patterns may be very narrow and rigid in their activities for fear of becoming overwhelmed; they won't go to certain restaurants, or will choose jobs that minimize sensory overload. Basically, the obsessive compulsive pattern manifests as a tendency to being negative, controlling, stubborn, rigid, and risk-averse. The rituals and obsessive thoughts are part of this overall pattern, which is why, in clinical literature, the obsessive compulsive personality was originally described as being perfectionist.

In contrast, individuals more prone to anxiety or even depression tend to get themselves into situations where they get anxious and panicky and overwhelmed because they don't anticipate, don't see the big picture, and don't try to control their environment as well. Whereas individuals with obsessive compulsive patterns try to do things on their own to prevent getting overwhelmed, anxious individuals get overwhelmed, helpless, needy, and to seek help from others to calm down. Individuals with obsessive compulsive patterns strive to be independent and control their environment and those around them. When they are dependent on others (which can often be the case), it's a controlling, demanding type of dependency, "Do this; do that," rather than, "I'm so overwhelmed; please help me!" It is a very different experience to deal with an obsessive compulsive individual as opposed to an anxious individual.

When trying to help an obsessive compulsive person, whether child or adult, it is important to understand these underlying dynamics, to realize that the individual is very anxious and the obsessive compulsive patterns are a response to anxiety. In fact, many of the same medications are used to treat both obsessive compulsive patterns and anxiety states.

Environments That Help Overcome Obsessive Compulsive Patterns

Now the question is: what are the aspects of an ideal environment for someone with obsessive compulsive patterns, so that pharmacologic treatment is either not needed, or is used only as part of an overall program that supports developing healthy coping strategies? The key is a multi-faceted approach.

Soothing Environments/Soothing Relationships

The most important element is to create, within the context of the person's primary relationship (i.e., with caregivers if the person is a child, or with the spouse or significant other for adults), a soothing, comforting environment. We want to explore with the individual the areas in which she is over-reactive to sensation, that is, instead of treating her obsessive thoughts or rituals as irrational, seeing them as clues to what she is over-reactive to.

For example, on the physical side of things, the person may be especially ritualistic or obsessive around eating, and it may because her sense of taste and smell are very hyper-reactive, and so eating is a particularly anxiety-provoking experience. She may be obsessive around sexual behavior because certain types of touch are overwhelming for her and she wants to control the experience. The obsessive behavior may be around the types of clothes she wears, or types of music she listens to.

On the other hand, the obsessive pattern may have to do with certain attitudes, feelings, or thoughts, rather than physical sensations that come from the outside. Individuals who are hyper-responsive in general are hyper-responsive to their own emotions as well. For example, fear of anger is common, because anger is associated with being out of control; anger propels one into actions that one can't always control. Ironically, obsessive individuals sometimes do get out of control when they get angry, and have tantrums even as adults, which only confirms for them the need for an obsessive compulsive coping strategy, rather than a more flexible approach.

So, we want to help people with obsessive-compulsive patterns recognize the situations and contexts in which they become anxious and feel overwhelmed, and offer them very soothing responses with a lot of nonverbal as well as verbal communication in these situations. For verbal children and adults, we want to help them describe their feelings of being overwhelmed in detail. As one child said, "My body is about to explode." An adult explained, "It feels like a thousand particles hitting my skin at the same time." People have some very interesting metaphors! This is something caregivers, family members, spouses, therapists, teachers, and good friends can do to help an obsessive compulsive person feel soothed. The key is to have a relaxed tone of voice, exchange soothing gestures, and give reassuring nods to make the person feel comfortable, rather than interrogated, as she describes the experience. Through this process, people can start to understand their own inner life; they can become very knowledgeable about what overwhelms them and what is at the core of their obsessive compulsive patterns.

Expanding the Range of Experience

Once the person is able to be soothed and to soothe herself more easily, we want to help her to develop a wider tolerance for different experiences. The way to do this is through gradual exposure to new situations with lots of soothing, nonverbal interactions, and lots of verbal exploration of feelings. We want to go at the person's own pace "one toe in the water at a time," rather than using the behavioral technique called implosion, in which, for example, you would put a person who is afraid of elevators in an elevator for four hours, hoping she will implode out the fear by getting exhausted and finally relaxing.

Developing Assertiveness

As the person expands her tolerance for a wider range of experience, we want to help her work on expressing assertiveness and constructive leadership, and on expressing anger in socially appropriate, constructive, grounded ways. The goal is for the person to be knowledgeable about anger, and then to evaluate its appropriateness in a situation and decide if it deserves mobilization into assertive statements, or whether it's simply a reflection of her own irrational fears. For example, if a wife feels angry at her husband, is this feeling a result of her own fears being triggered accidentally, or does she need to take action and have a serious discussion with her husband about things that he is doing?

In either case, of course, and as part of the process of figuring it out, the person should be able to discuss the anger with a close friend or spouse or therapist. But what she decides to do, or to demand as part of a negotiation, depends on the assessment of that anger. The first step is to become aware of the anger and the degree of it; this awareness helps keep the fear of getting out of control at bay. With this approach, we often see gradual improvement in the need for the obsessive compulsive patterns or ritualistic behavior.

With children who are preverbal or who have special needs, we want to work on as much of this as possible at the pre-language level. To the degree that we do Floortime and improve the back-and-forth communication with gestures, and negotiate different sensory environments and different social situations using gestures, we often encourage flexibility and creativity and see less ritualistic and repetitive behavior.

Addressing Physical Factors

Some individuals have motor planning and sequencing problems that contribute to their difficulty with regulating and soothing themselves. For both children and adults, we can improve motor planning and sequencing through various exercises, games, and activities. For children, these might include obstacle courses or treasure hunts. (Many ways to address motor planning and sequencing problems are covered in my other books, including *Engaging Autism and Building Healthy Minds.*) Sensory integration activities such as running, jumping, spinning, deep pressure, throwing, catching, kicking, balance exercises, and so forth, can improve relaxation and decrease ritualistic or repetitive behavior patterns. Physical exercise, improving muscle tone, and improving motor coordination give individuals more confidence in their bodies, which reduces the tendency to over-reactivity, panic, and feeling overwhelmed. Achieving this fundamental sense of physical security, coupled with more secure, soothing relationships, helps lessen the need for obsessive compulsive patterns. Activities such as yoga and meditation, that develop deep breathing and relaxation, can also be very helpful.

Nutritional Factors

Nutritional approaches are also useful to try before one considers medication. Basically, removing additives, preservatives, chemicals, processed carbohydrates, sugars, and fruit juices from the diet, as well as, for some individuals, specific food groups such as wheat products or dairy products, may be helpful. That is because sugars, processed carbohydrates that convert quickly to sugars, and chemicals often stimulate more epinephrine release (an "adrenaline rush") in the body. That release can overwhelm hyper-responsive individuals; it revs them up and makes them more over-vigilant and over-reactive, and intensifies their anxiety even though it feels good for the moment. So a chemical-free diet consisting of complex carbohydrates, lots of vegetables, lots of protein, and very chewy fruits (rather than fruit juices) creates a more even blood glucose level, which tends to help stabilize the person's mood and reactivity.

In summary, there are many things we can do to address obsessive compulsive disorders before resorting to pharmacologic interventions. Whether or not someone can benefit from a pharmacologic approach as well is determined by the amount of progress she is making with the kind of program described above. When using medication, you have to weigh the pros and cons, look for side effects, assess whether it is helping, and use it for the shortest term possible. We always like to recommend trying the approaches described above for at least six months before trying medications, to see what the individual's progress is like.

Overcoming Obsessive Compulsive Patterns: Two Examples

Case Study of a Child with Obsessive Compulsive Patterns

At three years old, Charlie was a finicky little boy who was already trying to control his world. He wouldn't go to preschool, fought over which socks and pants to wear (he only wanted soft cottons), would only play with certain children and not others, and battled his parents at every front. His parents came for a consultation because they were concerned about his negativity and their constant struggles with him.

We discovered that Charlie fit the classic obsessive compulsive pattern of being very over-reactive to sensation. His mother was a very anxious person who became hyper-reactive herself whenever Charlie challenged her. Meanwhile, Charlie's father was basically non-existent, and when he was home he was authoritarian and punitive and frightened Charlie enormously. We first addressed the family situation by getting the parents into counseling so that the mother could calm down and the father could be more available and less punitive. Both parents began doing several Floortime sessions a day with their bright, highly verbal child. They also created a very soothing environment at home.

Then we began a program of activities involving firm pressure and movement, which Charlie loved, to improve his sensory regulation, as well as working on his muscle tone and motor planning, which were a little weak. We also involved him in fantasy play in which he could be the boss, and we challenged him to assert himself. Gradually, we expanded his friendship base, starting with the kids he already liked, and then slowly adding another child who was a little rougher and a little less predictable.

Charlie had been taken out of preschool, but after six months we started him back in preschool for about 45 minutes a day, and gradually worked up to two hours. He tolerated this very well and actually, over time, became both assertive and, because he was sensitive and could tune into other children, somewhat of a leader. We discovered he had a remarkable sense of humor and could make the other kids laugh, and he became very popular among his peers. As his muscle tone and motor planning improved, he got into sports and began enjoying team activities. Now Charlie is a gifted teenager who is doing well both socially and academically and has a good, cooperative relationship with his parents.

Case Study of an Adult with Obsessive Compulsive Patterns

Margie, a 45-year-old mother working in computer sciences, found herself having lots of obsessive worries about her oldest daughter, who was about to go off to college. She was engaging in certain repetitive behaviors to help her feel that her daughter was safe; for instance, she would call her five times a day on her cell phone, or sometimes just dial her number and listen to her daughter's voice on the outgoing message. Margie knew her behavior was irrational, but she felt compelled to do it, even though it didn't reassure her and only made her feel more anxious.

We discovered that Margie had always been hyper-responsive to sensation, and in fact got into computers because it was a working environment she felt she could control. She had married a passive man, who basically allowed her to control him and would do everything she asked. He had the more maternal role in terms of being softer and more soothing, while Margie wanted to be in charge of everything. However, she hadn't anticipated the challenges of her first daughter, who in fact was very similar to her. The daughter was very bright, successful, social, and independent, but she was also controlling and sometimes negative. She was basically a secure, cautious person who was coping well within her personality structure and didn't really require mother's worry.

We looked at Margie's patterns and analyzed her hyper-reactivity and her current anxieties and fears. Because she was so controlling at home, but hadn't been very anxious in the past, her husband had pulled away from trying to be helpful and soothing to her. So we started off by helping the couple to connect more intimately, so the husband could soothe Margie and help talk her through her anxieties.

We then helped Margie acknowledge the fears that were underneath her need to control and to engage in obsessive behavior and worries. She was closer to her daughter than to anyone else in the family, even her husband, so she was afraid of losing her. And she was scared and overwhelmed by her own feelings. Margie was also, mostly at an unconscious level, very angry at her daughter for choosing a college away from home, because she wanted to be able to see her all the time, even though consciously she wanted her daughter to have an independent life. She needed to get in touch with her angry feelings, but was very scared of being overwhelmed by them and losing control.

We took essentially the same approach with Margie that we did with little Charlie, starting with creating a soothing environment for her. This involved helping her husband to take his rightful place as Margie's primary confidante, instead of their daughter, so he could support Margie at both the preverbal and the verbal level. She began therapy to learn to talk about her feelings, particularly her anger. And we helped her expand her sensory world to include more activities, rather than just her work and some very ritualistic hobbies on the computer. She had low muscle tone and poor coordination, so we got her involved in an exercise program. It turned out that Margie enjoyed ice skating, which is very good for muscle tone, balance, and coordination, so she started an ice skating program.

Working with these different elements, Margie improved dramatically over the course of a year, without the use of medication. She had in fact come in seeking medication for her "obsessive compulsive and anxious states," but it turned out she didn't require it once we addressed all the weaknesses on her developmental pathway that had created the problem in the first place. The advantage of this approach was that she became a stronger, more flexible, and more creative person in the process, in addition to having relief from her symptoms.

The above examples show the value of understanding an individual's developmental profile in addressing her disorder. Not every individual is as successful as Charlie and Margie were, but creating a program with these elements helps people with obsessive compulsive patterns, even when medication is also needed, begin a course of recovery that enables them to broaden their capacities and become more flexible individuals. The important thing to remember is that the symptoms should be seen as an opportunity for overall improvement and overall gains and flexibility.

Points to Remember

A comprehensive intervention for helping someone overcome OCD would include the following aspects:

- Determining the nature of the person's hyper-sensitivity–are they sensitive to physical sensations, or to their own thoughts and emotions?
- Encouraging the expression of the person's experience
- Expanding the person's range of comfort around sensations and experiences
- Developing the individual's ability to be assertive
- Exploring physical solutions, such as nutrition and exercise, to help the person self-regulate.

Chapter 9

Behavioral Disorders

In this chapter we'll consider children and adults with behavioral and conduct disorders—those individuals prone toward impulse control problems and extreme anti-social behavior, who have difficulty using good judgment when it comes to what should and shouldn't be done, and following the rules. Obviously, these disorders run the full gamut, from mild impulsivity, characteristic of many children, which may include pranks and maybe problems at school, to being aggressive or difficult, to major anti-social acts and illegal behavior that may appear during the teen years, but sometimes during the pre-teen years as well.

When we look at the developmental pathways leading to these problems, we see a very different pattern from what we've described for anxiety and depression. Children who ultimately manifest behavioral and conduct disorders develop very early in life the biological tendency to crave sensation. In other words, they crave a lot of sensory input. They're often very, very active, wanting more touch or more sound or more firm pressure, and especially more movement. We see little boys and little girls bump into people or run into things because they crave so much sensation, and often this is not understood by parents. As babies, these children may just be very active, but as toddlers they begin to move around a lot and get into hot water, knocking things over and being in places where parents don't want them to be. This invites several kinds of responses, particularly before the toddlers get to be verbal.

One response is that the caregiver becomes overwhelmed and freezes, providing no feedback at all—no guidance, no response. The other response is to become overly punitive, which frightens the child. Finally, a family environment can be disorganized, neglectful, or abusive, or, if a child has multiple caregivers (such as in a foster care situation), alternately caregiving and depriving. When the environment is severely undermining, we often see big-league delinquent and anti-social behavior later on. When there is a basically intact, loving family, children with this biologic tendency may show milder kinds of impulse control and behavioral and conduct difficulties.

During the first years of life, this type of sensation-craving child needs lots of back-and-forth interaction to help him slow down. So we can counter-regulate, beginning with matching his activity level by marching around the house with him, looking for that toy, going through the obstacle course, jumping over things, and seeing what makes noises. We want to do these activities together with the child, varying our speed from fast to medium-speed to slow and eventually to super-slow motion and back again. So we may bang on drums quickly with the child, at a moderate pace, slowly, and then back up to fast again. We can be soldiers or ballerinas together with the child—whatever scenario allows us to work with shifting rhythms from fast to slow, so the child becomes a better self-regulator. It's very important for this child to learn constructive ways to meet his need for sensation, such as sports, dance, or games that are action-oriented, but that also have structure and rules. In this way the child can meet his sensory-craving needs while at the same time being part of a regulated, constructive, socially meaningful activity and getting lots of positive feedback from his caregivers.

As the child progresses to the preschool years and fantasy play becomes possible, then the interaction with caregivers can have all kinds of adventurous themes that incorporate action: princesses who can fly or princes fighting dragons, for example. It's very important for the child with this type of biological tendency to verbalize feelings, especially feelings of disappointment or sadness, because the perception of these feelings by caregivers can be obscured by the child's sensation-craving, impulsive, action-oriented style. We want to look for opportunities to ask the child, "Oh, how did that feel?" to help the child slow down, reflect, and express himself. As children who crave sensation enjoy deep pressure, giving them firm massages—rubbing their backs, legs, or arms—can help them relax and focus on discussing their feelings, if prompted with empathetic questions.

The same pattern can work for adults as well: deep massage, soothing discussion, verbalizing feelings of sadness and disappointment, and helping them slow down when they're all hyped up. Sometimes this kind of interaction is stereotyped as "getting in touch with your feelings," but connecting with the underbelly or the softer side of life is very important for the action-oriented, impulse-ridden, trouble-making child, teenager, or adult. Developing this aspect of themselves is important, especially if they have experienced what we call the stone-faced type of caregiving, in which the parent tends to freeze in the face of strong emotion, or the punitive reaction. This only awakens more anger and humiliation and then leads, when coupled with sensory-craving, to more acting out as the child gets older.

The pattern we see, then, that leads to conduct disorders is often a pattern of a biologic tendency to crave sensation, with activity-craving as part of that, coupled with caregiving that doesn't counter-regulate or counter-balance very well. Instead of down-regulating, instead of providing the child with socially appropriate ways to be active and interactions that help teach him rhythmic movements encompassing the whole range of speed, the caregiver either freezes, which allows the child to stay out of control, or takes the punitive approach, which makes the child even more out of control in reaction. Then the behavioral problems escalate. This pattern appears in the adult environment, too, in terms of how families, spouses, friends, and the law enforcement establishment respond to basically decent people who could learn to be good citizens if we were better at counter-regulating and providing constructive environments, whether for teenagers from deprived backgrounds or for adults who are already manifesting ongoing impulse control problems.

A tendency toward craving sensation and unhelpful caregiver responses are not the only factors; social and cultural influences can also lead to conduct and behavioral problems. Although the pattern described above is characteristic, it isn't the only pathway toward antisocial behavior. Joining a rowdy, limits-testing group, sometimes a shy, passive, anxious child follows others and gets into trouble. Sometimes fearful, anxious children become daredevils or overly bold or impulsive to deal with their fears. There are other biologic tendencies, too; not all individuals with behavioral disorders fit the sensory-craving pattern.

Sometimes a hyper-sensitive, hyper-reactive child pushes or shoves, but for a different reason than the child who craves sensation.

Case Studies of Individuals with Behavioral Disorders

Following are two illustrations—one of a child and one of an adult—that show how this pattern plays out in real-life situations. These examples demonstrate how we were able to use developmental, family-oriented principles to help both the child and the adult become healthy individuals who were better regulated and felt better about themselves. When the environment causes humiliation and anger in an individual, depression and a negative self-image also result, which are compensated for by increasing the impulsive behavior, making the individual prone, sometimes, to substance abuse patterns, as well as acting out.

Case Study of a Child

We started working with Adam when he was about four years old. He was very active *in utero* and was moving from the time he was a few days old. His mother described Adam as a delightful baby who liked to wave his arms and move his legs. Once he got sitting up and crawling (he was early in his crawling) and, eventually, walking, he was a little fireball around the house. He was initially considered to be adorable because he explored everything. His mother noticed early on that he craved lots of sensory input; he liked to touch everything, see everything, play with everything in sight.

While little Adam had his mother's admiration, Adam's father was a stern disciplinarian who had grown up in a military family. Interestingly, he was a police officer who had risen through the ranks, turning his military upbringing to good professional use. Unfortunately, he tried to apply his stern, disciplinarian tactics to his dealings with his son. So, Adam's mother indirectly encouraged Adam's exploration and rambunctiousness, while his father was harsh and restrictive, and often frightened him with his angry yelling and sometimes also by holding and shaking him. (He was not physically abusive, but was physically restraining in a harsh manner.)

What's important with small children who crave sensation and who are on the impulsive side is to help them learn to signal with gestures and for the parents to inhibit the child's impulsivity through counter-gesturing. The idea is that with just a head nod or a stern look or a certain emotional expression, a parent can signal that the child's behavior is inappropriate, and the child gets it because he is a good emotional signaler and can read and respond to emotional signals.

However, Adam didn't have that experience. His mother was loving, but in a superficial way. She didn't want to get involved with conflicts or challenges, and showed no discrimination or shift in her emotional tone no matter what her son did. She had some help from a nanny with a similarly indulgent, avoidant personality, but the nanny often left Adam to his own devices to watch videos or roam around the house while the mother was off having lunch with friends or doing errands. Then, when Adam's father came home and saw the house in shambles, he would come down hard and institute punitive restrictions—time outs, insisting that Adam spend long periods of time sitting still in a chair—instead of interacting or working on developing a preverbal signaling system (or any kind of communication system) with his child.

As a toddler, Adam was an impulsive child who was getting increasingly aggressive and angry. Since his mother was out a great deal of the time and not very involved with him, nobody did pretend play with Adam, so he didn't learning the second way that children have of regulating their behavior, which is by turning their actions into ideas in imaginative play. Instead of playing out themes of exploration or adventure or even conflicts between good guys and bad guys so that he could elevate his actions to the world of ideas, Adam continued to act out and be impulsive. By this point, he was having tantrums and throwing and breaking things.

In preschool, Adam started acting out with other children: pushing, shoving, biting, and kicking whenever he didn't get his way. He was verbal and he seemed to learn quickly, but he was at the mercy of his impulses. As he went on through preschool, these problems only worsened and the parents started to get called in to the school. His father got more punitive, while his mother became anxious and defensive and kept changing schools. But each school gave her the same feedback.

Finally, when he was four, Adam was brought to see me. After taking a very detailed history and observing Adam on numerous occasions—at school, at home, and in my office—we validated the dynamic described above. For example, in the office, every time Adam got frustrated while playing, he threw a ball hard at Daddy or Mommy, tried to break toys, or tried to run out of the room. When his father got mad and yelled and physically restrained Adam, Adam got scared, but immediately thereafter would break something else even more viciously. So he turned his fear into more anger.

The first aspect of the comprehensive program we established was to help the parents begin working together as a team: teaching Adam's father to be more constructive in the way he set limits, getting the mother involved in a more intimate way with her son and his challenges, and getting the father home earlier in the evening (he didn't usually get home until 7:30) so he could spend time with his son. Each parent was to do three Floortime sessions a day with Adam, focusing on emotional signaling—being very animated and giving Adam lots of nonverbal, gestural feedback to inhibit him when he began to get impulsive, yet with nodding and admiring looks and gestures when he was playing constructively.

Another focus of the Floortime was marching to the beat of Adam's drum—playing out themes that he liked and accommodating his need for activity and sensation. We set up the home to support these needs, with swings and things to climb and slides and slosh pits filled with foam rubber that he could jump into. At the same time, we always gave his activities meaning and played out dramas. So, he would be Spider-man or a Teenage Mutant Ninja Turtle, and we'd help him embellish all the characters in the drama with motives. Since Adam was a very verbal child, we'd ask questions such as, "What did the bad guys do? What made them do that? What are the good guys trying to do? Who do you want to be today? Why?" Interestingly, Adam would always elect to be the good guy (albeit a very aggressive good guy); he didn't want to be identified as a bad guy. He would often make his father be the bad guy. We worked with Adam's father on softening his approach, and with each parent on playing out these pretend dramas with Adam individually. Eventually, we had dramas with all three, and the pretend dramas included a lot of gesturing.

Over time, with his parents' empathy and lots of back-and-forth communication, Adam was able to improve his emotional signaling system. He began to enjoy the make believe play because he could express his need to move around and satisfy his craving for sensation, yet he also learned to play within rules, which included not breaking anything or hurting anyone. Whenever Adam broke a rule, the play would undergo a time-out and stop. That alone was enough of a sanction, initially, to help him conform to the rules of the play sessions.

As this was occurring, the play themes began evolving and the characters had more complex motives. Eventually, when people were hurt, Adam, on his own, would bring in a surgeon to heal the person and themes of nurturing and caretaking entered the dramas, as well as themes of aggression and conflict. The male characters also started eating, and that evolved into occasional family dramas. We worked with the parents to help Adam explain why the characters felt the way they did, to encourage him to talk indirectly about his own feelings.

In addition to being coached periodically by me, because Adam's behavior had become so problematic, we had him doing one-on-one Floortime with a psychologist who specialized in working with young children. The psychologist was able to work with Adam's issues at a deeper level than Adam's parents could, and also provided ongoing coaching for the parents. This person also provided consultation to Adam's school, coaching the teachers to offer lots of guidance to Adam and to set firm boundaries and limits, but in a very supportive, non-punitive manner.

The parents had their own counseling sessions with the psychologist to address their own issues. The mother learned that her fear of being more intimate with her son came from her history of having a very superficial relationship with her own parents. With the psychologist's support, she gradually became more involved with Adam, beyond just admiring him. And the father explored his childhood fear of his own father, and how he came to believe that harshness was the only way to interact with children. As he became softer with Adam, he was able to mourn not having had that himself as a child, and, as a side-effect, became a more effective leader at work, because he could be compassionate as well as firm with his officers.

Over the course of the next three years, Adam gradually began doing better at school and forming peer friendships. He is now nine years old and the family is functioning well; we see them only for periodic follow-up sessions. He is an example of a child who originally would have been diagnosed, when we first saw him, with a conduct or behavioral disorder. However, by focusing on his underlying sensory processing pattern and on the family dynamics, and most importantly on what was missing in Adam's development (i.e., family intimacy, a signaling system that would allow him to read and respond to nonverbal cues to modulate and regulate his anger and aggression, and a fantasy life that could help him express feelings creatively rather than acting out), we were able to help Adam get back on course.

Case Study of an Adult

Eddie, a 42-year old man, shared some traits in common with little Adam. Eddie came to see me because he had been arrested for fighting in a bar with another patron; Eddie had hit the other person. It appeared to everyone that he had started the fight after some arguing. This was the third time Eddie had been arrested for physically fighting in various social settings, and the judge reluctantly gave him probation on the condition that Eddie begin therapy. He dutifully entered therapy, but less with internal motivation to change than with a desire to stay out of jail. However, he was verbal and willing to talk; his initial representation of himself was as a good citizen who held down a job.

However, he got into frequent arguments with people at work, too, often blaming the others (as he did in the barroom situations) for provoking him. He had all his aggressive behavior rationalized, always making other people at fault. His attitude was, "if you don't stand up for yourself, nobody else will." Eddie was married; his wife was very passive and let Eddie yell at her and control her. They had a new baby who, at 13 months, was passive and compliant so far. Eddie had very little to do with the child, except to brag that his son was a very "good baby" because he "listens to me and does whatever I want him to do."

As we explored Eddie's background, we learned that his father had left the family when Eddie was very young. His mother's behavior was inconsistent: sometimes she was very admiring and almost used her son as a replacement for her husband, building him up to heights that he couldn't possibly manage to achieve or fulfill; at other times, she was derogatory, critical, and negative. She didn't spend much time with Eddie because she was busy working, and she left in him in the care of various babysitters and daycare centers, some of which were chaotic and poorly run. She then married a man who turned out to be similar to her, vacillating between passivity and temper tantrums and actual physically abusive behavior—he would hit Eddie whenever the child misbehaved. Needless to say, there was very little emotional signaling going on, very little intimacy or empathy, and little opportunity for imaginative or pretend play.

Eddie's behavior problems started early on with the torturing of animals, which is very typical in the history of individuals with conduct disorders. He would collect insects and pull their legs off. Sometimes he would entice stray cats with milk and then throw things at them to see if he could scare them off. He reported this to me in our sessions with a mixture of glee at his cleverness and shame in his awareness that this was pretty sadistic and inappropriate behavior for a child. He frequently got into fights with other kids at school and was known as a "bad apple" around the playground, but he frequently got his way because he intimidated other kids. He was big for his age, well-coordinated, and a reasonably good athlete. He managed to get through school without getting into significant difficulties because of his large size and athletic skills.

Eddie went to college, where he played football and frequently got drunk, acted out, and got into trouble with the administration because of his fighting. He was put on probation a few times, but wasn't booted out of college, and he got a degree. At the time he came to see me, he had his own business running a bar. Some of his aggression, take-charge attitude, and lack of tolerance for anybody "disrespecting him" found some constructive expression in running a tight ship at work, although he did run into problems with his customers. Then, when he went out himself drinking at other establishments he got into trouble with this series of fights. He also occasionally got physical with his wife, and a number of times she was very close to calling the police but refrained from doing so.

As we reconstructed Eddie's past, we could see the developmental pathways that led to his having the challenges that he did. Like little Adam, Eddie had been a child who craved sensation, and with some experiences that would have helped him learn to modulate this tendency constructively, he could have been a successful athlete or entrepreneur, and probably had the qualities of leadership that would have helped him grow in any profession that he had chosen since he was also very bright and verbally articulate.

Eddie's therapist (someone whom we selected) worked with him in the same ways we would work with a child. He was very animated and gave Eddie lots of gestural feedback, but also helped him learn to put actions into words and to express feelings. Eddie had particular difficulty with feelings of weakness, passivity, disappointment, sadness, and loss—anything he couldn't compensate for by false bravado and a tough-guy attitude. He was also quite frightened, underneath it all, of his own anger and his ability to be destructive, which he compensated for by his bravado and the attitude that he would take no "shit" from anybody. Deep down, he harbored the idea that he had driven off his father because of his aggression as a child. Again, he covered this over by acting out the opposite, as many people do; he actually indulged himself in more aggressive behavior, idealizing himself as being a rough-and-tumble kind of person.

The therapist's posture towards Eddie was one of empathy and warmth, but also gentle confrontation about any hint of acting out, impulsive behavior, or the tough guy attitude in the therapy sessions. He asked Eddie questions such as, "Are you showing me the same kind of moxie that you like to show the world? What's the bravado covering up here?" He was always trying to get to the deeper, softer side of Eddie's personality. More important than the questions, initially, was the therapist's empathy and warmth and the fact that he didn't allow Eddie to get under his skin with provocative statements. Eddie tried to provoke the therapist by attacking the therapist's religion, his way of handling his office practice, fantasies about the way the therapist operated with his own wife, and other provocative statements that could get most therapists at least a little tense. We had deliberately selected someone who wouldn't get caught up in these kinds of dynamics.

In therapy, Eddie had a very different experience than he'd had when growing up. It was one of constant empathy and warmth, but also of firm confrontation when he began to act out, provoke, paid his bills late, came in a few minutes late for a session, or slammed the door a little harder than usual when closing it. These were all subjects for a great conversation and a lot of gestural feedback, such as raised eyebrows, and "What's going on here?" Now Eddie was in a relationship with someone who gave him lots of feedback at the gestural and verbal levels and helped him elaborate his feelings into words, particularly the difficult feelings having to do with loss, disappointment, humiliation, and sadness, as well as expressions of anger and the real fears Eddie had around anger. He was afraid that it would drive people off and that he would lose relationships just like he lost his father.

About two-thirds of the way through his therapy, Eddie actually searched out his biological father and they were able to have a rapprochement and begin a relationship. Eddie's father, by this time, was retired. He had been working as a laborer in a construction firm and had had an alcohol abuse problem, but was now doing reasonably well. Eddie began nurturing him a little bit as he was living in a retirement community with his current wife.

Over time, Eddie became a softer, more compassionate individual and developed some awareness of the roots of his aggression. He was still prone to having his "blood boiling over," but was able to contain and curb it and remind himself that deeper feelings of humiliation were fueling the anger. He also became more aware of the fear of loss that fueled his anger and the rage he had at his father as sources of some of the abusive behavior he was evidencing as an adult. In follow-up sessions after Eddie had completed his therapy, we observed that he was functioning well. His child was now older and all his relationships were better. His businesses were more successful and he hadn't gotten into trouble with customers or in his own recreational behavior in the last few years.

These examples of Adam and Eddie illustrate similar principles that help with behavior problems: working on the preverbal gesturing system, putting feelings into words and into fantasies, and getting in touch with and expanding the range of feelings the person can tolerate, particularly in the realm of difficult feelings.

Points to Remember

Principles that help prevent or overcome behavioral problems at any age include the following:

- Finding appropriate, constructive outlets for physical energy and the need for sensation
- Developing the preverbal gesturing system
- Learning to put feelings into words and express them creatively, through play or creative endeavors
- Getting in touch with and expanding the range of feelings the person can tolerate, particularly in the realm of difficult feelings.

Chapter 10

Borderline Personality Disorders

The term "borderline syndrome," also known as "borderline disorder" or "borderline personality disorder," is confusing. It is sometimes used in a derogatory way, as in, "Oh, he is borderline!"—meaning the person is hard to read, hard to understand, different. Now we'll take the mystery out of the concept of "borderline" and explain what clinicians mean when we use that term. This helps anyone in relationship with people characterized in this way to have a deeper appreciation of what these individuals are struggling with and how they can be helped.

Going back to our developmental model, let's look at the pathway to this challenge so we can better understand the characteristics of borderline disorders. The fifth stage in human development is the ability to create ideas or images (technically called representations or symbols). At this stage we can picture emotions and experience them in terms of their multiple features from many perspectives, including visual, tactile, verbal, and emotional (or feelings), at the same time. Then we reach the critical sixth stage, which is creating bridges between ideas. At this stage, if you ask a child why she wants to leave the dinner table, she'll say, "Because I'm bored!" This ability to build bridges between symbols or ideas allows us to link emotions together—our representations of emotions with someone else's. This is where we see the primary problem in borderline syndromes or borderline disorders.

The sixth stage is when we develop our ability to picture in a multisensory way our own feelings and the feelings of a caregiver (for a child) or the feelings of a partner or spouse or a good friend (for an adult). This ability enables us to do two things. First, it allows us to know who we are as a person because we experience ourselves as a group of feelings or a kind of vibrancy or tone in our bodies. We define ourselves by a whole range of feelings that characterize us, as well as thoughts, values, intentions, and experiences, but these are organized around our feelings. We also characterize others in this way. Our mom is experienced with a certain feeling tone, our dad in another way, and a good friend in yet another way.

Therefore, what brings us in contact with others and helps us understand them is this ability to build bridges between our feelings and their feelings. It also allows us to separate ourselves from them so we don't get confused between what's "us" and what's "them." We all get confused about this a little bit; we do what we call projecting or externalizing, where we put our feelings onto someone else. We interpret their actions based on what we are feeling. We also take things personally. If someone is angry, we often assume he's angry at us, or if someone else is scared, we assume she's scared of us.

The ability to have a sense of ourselves as more or less separate from others, to have a self-image or self-picture and, eventually, an identity that's distinct and defined, is based on the ability to connect ideas together because we can then connect our ideas to someone else's ideas and understand the differences between them. This is critical because without that we would constantly lose the sense of who we are and would confuse our feelings with others' feelings. Are we angry or are they angry? We may so over-identify with someone who's depressed that we feel depressed if we're near that person, and we don't know if we're depressed ourselves or just catching that person's depression. In such a case, we have poor physical and psychological boundaries, or a weak identity. This is the reason a teenager goes along with the group, even when she knows that what the group is doing is wrong or unwise. The weaker the sense of identity, the weaker the self-definition, the easier it is to become part of something else. We are all more or less likely to have this tendency; it's not a distinct phenomenon.

The second function of the ability to connect ideas together is that it allows us to relate the past to the present. The history of our lives and our feelings can be connected to the current moment, as in, "I'm angry because last year everyone forgot my birthday and this year it's happening again!" or, "I'm happy because this year I'm getting the present I wanted last year and didn't get." And as we get older, we can connect the past and present to the future; even young children can appreciate the idea of tomorrow or next week or their next birthday or the next holiday. Making connections between ideas starts between ages two and three, and reaches a crescendo when (at about age three) we can begin thinking causally. We no longer exist solely in the sea of creative feelings that characterize the fifth stage.

As this ability to connect ideas together improves, our sense of self and of others—a sense that incorporates the past, present, and future—grows. In other words, we develop a wider range of feelings, experiences, and intentions. These include fears and anxieties as well as happiness, assertiveness, curiosity, and creativity. We become complex people, situated within the context of the passage of time, existing in relationship to others. Eventually, as we get older, we exist in terms of a larger group: first, our peer group, then our community and country, and then work and relationships and the families we create. It keeps broadening as we move on in life, ideally encompassing the worldwide human family.

This sense of self and of others keeps growing and developing with experience, but only if the fundamentals are in place. If the fundamental capacity to connect ideas together is weak, then this edifice we're creating of a complex sense of self and a complex sense of others isn't as differentiated, stable, and secure as it might be. We want this sense of self and others to be broad and integrated, yet also distinct and unique to us and our experiences. As we connect to the larger spectrum of humanity, we still retain the sense of being a distinct individual. Then this sixth stage, this ability to connect ideas together, can evolve to incorporate the ability for multi-causal thinking, comparative thinking, gray-area thinking, and true reflective thinking throughout the life cycle.

In this developmental context, individuals characterized as having borderline syndrome tend to be vulnerable in their capacity to build bridges between ideas or representations, which means between feelings, and between past, present, and future, and between their sense of self and a sense of others. Sometimes we describe it as body boundaries that are less differentiated, less secure, and less stable. But we can think of it more specifically in terms of the capacity to connect ideas together. The ability exists, but it is easily overwhelmed by a storm of strong feelings. So when the person experiences extreme anger, sadness, fear, or sometimes even extreme intimacy with someone else, the intensity of the feeling overwhelms the ability to connect ideas together.

Individuals with this challenge, who don't have a secure ability to connect ideas together, often describe feelings and experiences that reflect this porous boundary. It may be that they become overly suspicious and worried that someone is angry at them, or someone is going to hurt them. It's not a chronic pattern like a person who always believes the FBI is after her; it's more of a temporary perspective related to the intensity of the feeling. It might be characterized by a depression or overwhelming sense of sadness when a loved one is sad. The individual puts herself in the other person's shoes and over-identifies with him or her, taking in that sadness and making it her own to a greater degree than the other person's original feeling. We all do this to some extent. If our spouse is ill our imagination may run wild with all kinds of dire outcomes, but an individual who has trouble connecting ideas together is unable to step back and say, "Gee, I'm really reacting strongly to this." Instead she would tend to believe that the world is coming to an end because the other person's situation is so upsetting to her.

Borderline syndrome might also manifest as a debilitating fear of success. We can all get anxious when good things happen too quickly and we're afraid we can't live up to certain standards, but, again, the typical person can step back, take a deep breath, and say, "Well, I'll do my best." Whereas the individual with borderline syndrome becomes convinced that she won't be able to perform and is paralyzed by anxiety. Again, this porous body boundary is based on a difficulty with connecting ideas together, particularly when feelings become very, very strong.

This challenge also results in misreading signals, which can lead to impulsive or inappropriate behavior. For example, a young adult may be in a new social situation at a club or bar and be unable to connect ideas together very well. If someone teases her, she may misread it and think the other person is trying to pick a fight. She may impulsively slap the other person, not because she's violent or aggressive, but because she wants to protect herself and can't distinguish between teasing and an actual threat of attack. So, impulsive behavior, anxiety, fear, depression, or suspicion can all be characteristics of a borderline personality. In addition, the same individual could vacillate, showing features of each of these at different times. There may be a dominant tendency toward more impulsive, depressive, suspicious, or fearful types of feelings. The key distinction with this disorder is in the nature of the experience. Rather than retaining a sense of reality and talking themselves through the exaggerated feelings, individuals with borderline disorder instead get lost in the feeling and see the emotion of the moment as reflecting the whole picture.

Therefore, the individual's sense of reality (what is sometimes called reality testing) is compromised. This temporary compromise in reality testing characterizes what is ordinarily diagnosed as borderline. This should be distinguished from a person who has a chronic and persistent difficulty with appreciating reality, which we often describe with different terms, such as psychotic or schizophrenic, or other types of deficits in reality testing on a more chronic basis. We're not talking about individuals who are delusional or who have an ongoing (constant) difficulty with appreciating reality. We're talking about people who experience temporary storms of this lowered ability to appreciate reality. That enables them or causes them to be more moody, impulsive, anxious, or fearful, and so forth.

Because of this, obviously, their relationships can be difficult and stormy. They can experience intimacy and closeness too intensely, then they pull away, but are afraid to be alone so they go back into the relationship. They can also cling in a dependent way, like a baby, feeling fear of abandonment as though the other person is going to leave them forever, even if the other person is just going away for a couple days on a business trip. This disorder obviously also affects relationships with colleagues, friends, family, and romantic relationships. At the same time, individuals characterized as borderline, as distinct from individuals having severe personality disorders (which we'll address later), tend to want relationships and like to be involved in lots of them, so the capacity for engaging and relating to others can be strong.

Sometimes people with borderline personality disorders are very charismatic. One woman with this disorder, because of her ability to "enter the skin" of another person, as well as her verbal skills and her overall sophistication, could seem to become different people. She didn't have multiple personalities with different names and identities—she knew she was the same person in some way—but she could be whoever anyone wanted her to be, to such a degree that she lost herself in others' expectations and views. Because of that she was good at making friends, and the initial months of her romantic relationships were often very intense because she was each man's perfect partner; she was whatever they wanted her to be. The men would be thrilled to find someone who so greatly shared their interests, who appreciated their particular wisdom and intelligence, and so forth. But then she would find herself very anxious, depressed, needy, and clingy because she'd basically lost her sense of who she was, and she'd be confused about what she was feeling and what her partner was feeling, and the relationship would fall apart.

Another woman had the opposite tendencies. She had trouble forming intimate relationships because she could so easily get inside the thoughts and feelings of others that it made her anxious and scared of losing who she was. So she'd start to pick fights and become stubborn and negative, sabotaging her relationships, even the potentially very good ones, in their early stages.

Another tendency for people with borderline syndrome is to be so fearful of being rejected and convinced that they will be rejected that they become demanding and clingy and frighten people away. One young man became so suspicious and jealous that if his girlfriend gave any indication of interest in another man, even if was just to point out what a good dancer he was or that he looked like a mutual friend of theirs, it would so threaten him that he would get angry and accuse his new girlfriend of being unfaithful, right after they discussed having an exclusive relationship. This would, obviously, drive the new partner away. Again, the common denominator in individuals with this challenge is the lapse of appreciation of reality and the fundamental weakness in this ability to connect ideas together.

Biological Tendencies

On the physical side, individuals with this pattern tend to have difficulties in the way they react to sensation. Many are over-reactive to sensation, so their feelings are more intense and therefore harder to contain within normal boundaries. Some, however, can be a little under-reactive and therefore can't organize their feelings well and connect them to others because they don't sense the feelings enough. Borderline personalities can have either tendency, but we see more of the over-reactive pattern. Motor planning and sequencing—the ability to create and organize patterns—tends to be problematic also. At the heart of the borderline syndrome is difficulty with maintaining stable patterns in terms of a sense of oneself and others, so the ability to sequence and link ideas together to create patterns may be weaker.

Visual-spatial thinking tends to be especially vulnerable in such individuals. Visual-spatial capacities are associated with big-picture thinking. Connecting all our feelings and images together into a sense of self involves big-picture thinking, whereas getting lost focusing on each detail means that we may be able to identify a hundred different feelings, but can't necessarily create the stable sense of self that requires incorporating all our feelings into an overall picture. Here, again, though, people vary somewhat—they may have only a weakness in visual-spatial thinking and not be too extreme in terms of reactivity to sensation, for example.

Interestingly, many individuals with borderline patterns can have very, very strong auditory processing and language skills and are considered extraordinarily intelligent by ordinary standards; they may do very well in school because of their excellent memory and good verbal and writing skills. But sometimes that area can be weak, also, which therefore can make the difficulty even more complex and perhaps more challenging to work with.

Thus, there can be a variety of sensory processing, motor planning, and sequencing challenges in this profile. However, the prototype is someone who is over-reactive to sensation, highly verbal, intelligent, and very sensitive, but who's weaker in terms of visual-spatial and motor planning and sequencing abilities, even if she has some excellent fine motor skills or even some excellent gross motor skills.

Then, in terms of the developmental scale, because their early regulation and sense of security is weak, their ability for engagement may be very strong, but chaotic, and they may find some feelings scary and difficult to deal with, especially aggression, assertiveness, and extreme intimacy. They may be gifted in short-run sequencing and problem-solving, but big-picture thinking and long-term strategizing are more difficult. The creative use of ideas is very strong, with many feelings represented, but creative dramas tend to stay more fragmented, with different emotions spinning around rapidly, rather than a more gradual exploration of each emotion and a bridging between them. In sum, we may have a very creative, but fragmented, person.

The critical ability to connect ideas together exists; individuals with borderline personality disorder may be able to answer "why" questions from an intellectual perspective, and be good causal thinkers and even very good multi-causal, gray-area, and comparative thinkers. They can give many reasons for something, compare A to B and think in shades of gray, and even give a sophisticated contextual analysis, perhaps. Under intense feelings, these higher thinking capacities are weaker and the person falls into more fragmented patterns, not so much polarized perspectives as piecemeal ones.

Finally, the ability for reflective thinking, or thinking in two frames of reference at one time ("Why am I so worried about my husband going away for the weekend? It shouldn't be a big deal…") can and often does occur for mild feelings' However, when feelings get intense that ability gets lost as part of the larger and more fundamental loss of the appreciation of reality.

Helping Individuals with Borderline Syndrome

Given the developmental pathway and regulatory profile for what we call borderline syndrome, what's the best way to be of assistance to a family member, friend, student, colleague, spouse, or patient who shows these characteristics? Even with this problem, such individuals often have special characteristics—a kind of "plus" factor—that others don't bring to our lives, qualities that energize us and make us feel wonderful so we want that relationship to work. We want to help the person grow, just as we hope he helps us grow.

The key is to pay attention to the developmental pattern we've described, because the pattern begins with uncertainty about self-regulation, particularly around strong feelings. In terms of the first developmental stage, it's very important to establish a sense of security in the relationship, whether it's a therapeutic or personal relationship, based on an understanding of the person's regulatory profile. If the person is over-reactive to sensation, we need to provide a lot of soothing. When the person has a storm of feelings and becomes unrealistic, we don't react and get lost in that ourselves. It's best to stay calm, with an attitude that expresses, "Let's calm down first then we can think this through." In other words, we don't join the drama, don't throw fuel on the fire, and don't argue with people with this profile when they're in the middle of an irrational storm. (This is good advice when dealing with anyone, because we can all get temporarily caught up in strong emotions, but it's especially important when interacting with someone who does this chronically and really gets lost in it.) Try to maintain the sense of security and maintain the relationship; don't react in kind. Don't pull away if they're rejecting; don't counter-attack if they're angry; and don't be impulsive if they're impulsive. Instead, be soothing, with an attitude of "let's calm down," and if they're reacting to a lot of noise and sensation, make the environment quieter.

Then, in terms of emotional signaling, focus on the emotion instead of the content. Don't pay so much attention to what they're saying (i.e., "You've been bad, you hurt my feelings, you're rejecting me," and so forth). Pay attention to the larger scope of the feeling—perhaps the person is worried about being abandoned, for example. Empathize with the feeling and try to create a reassuring atmosphere so the reality of that feeling is not reinforced, but rather is put in a more realistic context. But empty words won't do the trick; it's the reassuring tone of voice, the empathetic gestures, the understanding facial expressions, along with a continuing presence, all within the context of a slower, soothing, reassuring rhythm of back-and-forth emotional signaling. Based on the person's feeling, we can try to problem-solve with him and help him feel a little better and get through the current storm working as a team.

At the level of creating ideas, we want to help the person characterize her experience in new ways by focusing on the feelings and not the specific content of the worry—looking at the whole forest instead of getting lost in the trees. Perhaps she's worried about being abandoned or being criticized. We can help her to creatively put the feeling into words.

Eventually we can progress to connecting ideas together as part of problem-solving, helping the person understand what brought on the feelings, what the feelings are connected to, and why she is so scared of being left or of being attacked or so depressed over a friend's illness, for example. In a reassuring, supportive way, we help her take a step away and look at things. We're not trying to identify deep unconscious patterns (i.e., "Oh, you wanted to attack your mother so now you're afraid everyone's going to attack you."). Rather, we use the Socratic method to help the person connect patterns together. Any historical insights can come gradually as the person wonders about the past and sees how early patterns are connected to current patterns. Gradually, over time, what often happens is that higher levels of thinking emerge, even under intense feelings. The person begins thinking in two frames of reference at the same time and becomes able to take a step outside and observe herself.

This happens only very gradually, maybe over years in a long-term therapeutic, intimate, or family relationship. The important thing is to maintain a sense of security in the relationship and empathy in interaction around the feelings, so we create a very stable, secure, nurturing environment where integration (being in lots of feelings) and differentiation (distinctness and stability of developmental experiences) can be enhanced over time.

Therapeutically, medications are sometimes used to help diminish the intensity of overwhelming feelings, but these should only be prescribed by a very experienced clinician who really understands the patient's core issues. Some medications can make matters worse and intensify certain problematic feelings or lead to more fragmented thinking or diminish the creativity or intimacy in a relationship.

Earlier, we had an example of a very creative woman who entered the shoes of everyone she became involved with, and did well for the first few months of every relationship and then became anxious, depressed, suspicious, and clingy. She did very well over a 10-year period by seeing an empathetic therapist three times a week. The therapist created the conditions described above, and after about three years, the woman was able to form a stable relationship with a young man who truly loved her and who also provided these same experiences. Because he was somewhat under-reactive, he thrived on her intensity and emotionality, and was available enough to be empathetic and interactive without getting consumed. He was a big-picture thinker, very gentle and soothing, and could be reflective. However, the young woman would not have been attracted to this man before having several years of therapy, and it's unlikely he would have been able to hang in there as he did if the woman hadn't been in therapy.

It's hard for family members, friends, and romantic partners to be as helpful as they might be to people with borderline syndrome, because they can get caught up in the individual's strong feelings and become reactive, and therefore the relationship falls apart. But the therapist who's trained to understand such patterns can often provide the type of stable environment necessary to help the individual overcome the negative effects of borderline personality disorder–to make sure the person inner security blanket is holding strong.

Points to Remember

Helping individuals overcome borderline personality syndrome is a long-term process, characterized by the following components:

- Establishing a sense of long-term security, to promote self-regulation–rather than throwing fuel on the fire
- Empathizing with the feelings, rather than focusing on the content of the person's statements
- Helping the person connect ideas by asking questions

Chapter 11

Severe Personality Disorders

Severe personality disorders are related to borderline patterns but are very different in many respects. People with severe personality disorders may be chronically suspicious or chronically aloof and avoidant or chronically passive or chronically dependent, but they share the common feature of being unable to embrace certain emotional experiences. Many of their defenses or coping strategies lead to mild compromises in their appreciation of reality, although in a very different way than we described for borderline syndrome.

Personality disorders are a confusing topic to professionals and nonprofessionals alike. They are different from many other mental health disorders, such as anxiety and depression, which have clear symptoms. For example, people can generally tell if they are depressed or anxious because they are negative or they feel worried. But someone who has a personality disorder is by definition often unaware of his own tendencies. Rather than being an emotional state, a personality disorder is a way of relating to the world that is characterized by being limited or constricted. It's a narrow way of engaging the world.

Varieties of Severe Personality Disorders

One type of personality disorder is the passive-dependent personality. A person with this disorder approaches the world in a passive and dependent way and has a hard time, or finds it impossible to assert himself and to take initiative. He expects things to be done for him and depends a great deal on others. Unless somebody spoon-feeds him and nurtures him along, he finds it hard to cope. The narrowness of his passive, needy, dependent style of relating to the world eliminates many horizons relating to assertiveness, initiative, creativity, and adventure, and it often means that age-appropriate relationships are out of reach unless a partner can carry him along.

Then there is the sociopathic or antisocial personality, the person whose whole life is organized around not obeying the rules, around being exploitative and treating people as objects.

The schizoid personality is uncomfortable with intimacy and relationships and so isolates himself, spending huge amounts of time alone. This person finds relating to others extremely difficult and often anxiety-provoking.

Someone with a paranoid personality disorder is very suspicious, always thinks that others have hidden motivations and agendas, and may worry that people are out to get him. The difference between a paranoid personality disorder and an all-out distortion of reality is in the degree. Someone who believes the FBI is chasing him when there's no basis for that in reality, and therefore operates his life accordingly, is probably delusional. Someone with a paranoid personality may have all kinds of odd beliefs and may operate in a very cautious, suspicious, restricted way, but doesn't quite live in that belief system to the degree that a delusional person does.

Another common personality disorder is narcissism. The term, in a technical sense, refers to an individual who is very caught up in himself (like Narcissus, who fell in love with his own reflection in the pond). This preoccupation with the self may take many forms—people who talk constantly about themselves or who can't easily empathize with others—they can only see the world in terms of how it affects them. People with narcissistic personality disorders can often be very entertaining and engaging, initially, because their goal is to get you to like them or to see them in a certain way, or to be center-stage. They act in a way that charms others into focusing on them.

In the early years of our practice, we found certain children with whom we worked extremely likeable. We could engage them very readily. We felt that they liked the playroom and they liked us and we liked them, and this is after we'd known them for just a few minutes. As we got to know them better, we realized that many of them had problems in the narcissistic realm—they were extremely self-centered. Then we realized that they were very good at charming people. We began using that sense of quickly being charmed as an antenna to see whether narcissism was part of their make-up, though this tendency may not yet have been so severe as to be their primary way of engaging the world. Often, children don't have fixed personality disorders, they have emerging personality patterns, which are very flexible and can be favorably influenced.

Many adults, too, have tendencies towards one or another personality disorder. These tendencies can still be influenced by therapy, or by good relationships with family members, peers, or colleagues. One can sometimes develop a kind of sixth sense when it comes to narcissistic personality disorders. There are people whom we initially like very much, and then we realize that actually they're deliberately charming us, almost like a con man or woman. The very ease with which we like them is the tip-off that they have the narcissistic tendency.

Other personality disorders include: the depressive personality, who has a chronically gloomy perspective on the world; the anxious personality, with a chronically fearful perspective; and the obsessive-compulsive personality, who is preoccupied with control, neatness, orderliness, and detail. People with these personality disorders are more likely than people with other personality disorders to develop acute symptoms.

The Development and Prevention of Personality Disorders

Each of the personality disorders described above, as well as others, exists on a continuum from a pattern that's part of a person's make-up and falls in the normative range (because we can all have a little bit of depressive, obsessive, or anxious patterns in our make-up), to mild, moderate, or severe disorders. Many of us have moderate tendencies in one direction or another. Certain characteristics may actually be very good for certain careers; for example, a moderate tendency toward narcissism may be very good for those in the acting profession. They love entertaining, being admired, and getting up on stage, which in fact may be what prompted them to choose that profession in the first place.

The key is to understand how these different personality tendencies emerge from early life and what to do when you want to help someone, or you want to help yourself, become more flexible and overcome the mild to severe elements of the disorder and learn to adapt to a wider range of situations. The challenge with personality disorders—whether mild or severe—is that they limit one's way of engaging the world, whether in terms of intimacy, empathy, assertiveness, creativity, or flexibility to take on and enjoy new situations. (For a more complete description of each of these personality types, see the *Psychodynamic Diagnostic Manual,* available from www.icdl.com, which includes a full description of each of these personality types, as well as a little bit about their development.)

Let's look at how these personality patterns and disorders develop and then at some general principles of how we can help individuals make corrections. As we've said earlier, the first aspect to look at is the physical or constitutional factors that contribute to the disorder. Each of the severe personality disorders has a somewhat different pattern. For example, someone with an anxious personality disorder tends to be over-reactive to ordinary sensations, like touch and sound, which leads to the cautious, anxious thought and behavior patterns. Paranoid patterns tend to be associated more with hyper-responsiveness to the environment. People with this pattern are picking up cues all the time and being overwhelmed by them, and then are interpreting the cues in a fixed way, in the context of a theory, rather than simply thinking, "I'm just sensitive," or "I'm getting overloaded." The schizoid personality disorder, on the other hand, tends to be a more on the under-reactive side. This person is hard to rouse into relationships, is solitary, and can be in his own fantasy world.

Each of the types may also differ in their relative processing and motor planning strengths. For example, phobic individuals don't have a great deal of confidence in their bodies and often have motor planning and sequencing and visual-spatial processing challenges, along with over-reactivity to sensation. The important thing, when trying to help someone else with a limiting personality tendency, is to look at the person's sensory processing pattern. Are sensations overwhelming? Are there some sensations the person seeks out? Does the person tend to be under-reactive and require others to rouse him? Is he better verbally or visually? Can he plan and sequence many actions in a row, or is that hard? Determining the sensory-processing profile is the first step.

The developmental pathway for these personality disorders includes a relatively successful mastery of the core milestones—paying attention, engaging with others, exchanging simple gestures, doing some shared social problem-solving, using ideas to some degree creatively, and reaching some stage of logical thinking. However, development goes awry in two ways. First, at each of these stages, the experience that's embraced tends to be very constricted or narrow. So, when the individual is learning to gesture, express emotions, and read other people's emotions, he's often doing it in a narrower realm of emotional experience than would be typical.

Passive-dependent individuals, for example, often have an early childhood history in which assertiveness, curiosity, and creativity were not part of his agenda, so they weren't part of his shared social problem solving with his parents. He wasn't taking Mommy and Daddy by the hand and exploring the house, he was a little more passive and a little more dependent. Similarly, someone with an anxious personality disorder was cautious and lacking assertiveness as a child, shying away from competitive activities and boisterous peers. The depressive person often had a hard time embracing optimism, adventure, and a "can-do" attitude when he was young.

Because the defining aspect in the development of severe personality disorders is a narrowing of the emotional range the child can bring to the table, so to speak, the correction—whether in childhood or adulthood—is, obviously, to broaden that range. So, for example, if we see a passive, dependent tendency in a child, we can try challenge the child to be more assertive. We might tempt him to take more initiative by saying he can have the toy he wants, but he has to search for it or race us to get it. The key is to get the child involved and enjoying the thrill of mastery, as opposed to just letting him be passive because it's nice when he's quiet and sweet and doesn't bother us. With the older child it may mean spending a lot of time with a parent playing sports or doing an art project or participating in a hobby, like astronomy or cartooning or learning magic together, in which we set up situations where the child can experiment with competition safely. Then he will feel more comfortable being assertive with peers. Whatever the activity, we want to broaden that range of emotional experience gradually and systematically in a way that's enjoyable for the individual.

Of course, in doing so, we want to take into account the person's physical differences. If the child is over-reactive, we have to be soothing and very gradually help him be confident in his body. If he's under-reactive and more of a couch potato, we have to put a lot of energy into our interactions and can't take his under-reactivity as rejection or disinterest, but as a signal to be more energetic in the way we engage and more enticing in the way we draw him into the activity. Getting the child involved in more energetic activities also helps counteract the trend towards childhood obesity, which results in part from the more passive lifestyle of children these days where they sit in front of TVs and computers instead of running around the neighborhood with other children.

If, on the other hand, we see a child becoming more suspicious and cautious—the seeds of a later paranoid pattern—we ask what the child's relationship with his parents is like. Why is there a lack of trust and confidence? Ask the same thing with fearful or anxious individuals. Where is that anxiety and fear coming from? What experiences can help the child broaden his emotional range?

We want to do all we can to broaden the child's range of emotional experience, taking into account his sensory processing and motor planning abilities, and we also want to work directly on strengthening those abilities. Many children need special programs to develop motor planning and sequencing; these programs might include obstacle courses, athletics or dance, or moving in sequence to music. Many children also need gradual exposure to the sensations that are overwhelming, in the context of activities that help them regulate themselves. Bear hugs and deep pressure and different movement patterns can help a child keep from being overwhelmed in an environment where there is a lot of noise and activity going on.

Strengthening visual-spatial and verbal abilities is also important. The book, *Thinking Goes to School*, by Hans Furth and Harry Wachs, contains a series of exercises to strengthen visual-spatial thinking that can be incorporated into games and other activities. To help strengthen verbal abilities, have the child explain the games.

There are many ways in which we can help children expand their emotional patterns while taking into account their sensory and motor differences. But it's never too late to help teenagers, young adults, or even middle-aged adults, too. People in relationships with such individuals, and such individuals themselves, can help if they have an awareness of the narrowness of the pattern. The process is always the same—gradually broadening the range of emotional experiences.

We can help the person get in touch with feelings out his normal range directly by asking questions and talking about the challenging emotions, and indirectly by encouraging him to try new experiences in which his feelings are likely to be stirred up. Then we talk with the individual about it (with the support of the therapist, if necessary).

For a person who's passive and avoidant, we might say, "You know, I've noticed that you never get involved in a competitive sports activity—why is that?" "Well, it's too scary for me." "Well, what made you decide to give into that fear? Did you ever consider doing something you find a little bit scary, but not too scary?" Then the person might say, "I could try bowling; that's not as scary as other sports," and then, with our support, he might actually get involved in a bowling league or some other activity that's fun but that also has a competitive edge. Similarly, for the person who avoids relationships or intimacy, we can challenge him to be a little more patient and give relationships a little more time before deciding they're not for him. At the same time he's exploring the scary feelings associated with intimacy.

So the way to help prevent or overcome personality disorders is to address the person's predominant way of engaging the world, whether the tendency is mild, moderate, or severe, and also to look at the other side of the equation—the experiences that are avoided to maintain that narrow way of engaging the world. What aspect of emotional experience is not being embraced? Is it assertiveness? Is it curiosity? Is it intimacy? Is it vulnerability? The solution to a personality disorder is in broadening the emotional spectrum and embracing a wide range of experiences, taking into account the person's physical make-up and strengthening the processing patterns, particularly in childhood where they're more flexible, but also in adulthood.

Of course, some of the more severe personality disorders, like the paranoid personality or the schizoid personality, can border into unrealistic perceptions of the world, and individuals with these patterns often require long-term therapeutic relationships to effect a gradual change. Others may respond more quickly; a mild depressive or obsessive personality pattern may respond very quickly to either treatment or just life experiences that offer the therapeutic ingredients described above. In either case, growth involves relationships that help the person master each of the stages of emotional development, broaden his range of emotional experience, and master sensory and motor processing abilities that may be limited.

Finally, it is important to note that the more severe the pattern, the less likely the individual is to progress in a broad way much beyond the first level of causal or logical thinking in the developmental stages. People who get stuck at the first level of causal thinking and just get into a little bit of multi-causal thinking and don't really see shades of gray or nuances and subtleties tend to be more rigid or more polarized in their worldview. Certainly, a severe paranoid disorder or a schizoid disorder would tend to correlate with a fixed worldview. Obsessive-compulsive or anxious patterns both have an all-or-nothing view of the world—that the world is dangerous—so there isn't a lot of gray-area thinking. Even if the person is able to do gray-area thinking and even reflective thinking in the intellectual arena, in the emotional and social areas of life the person may be locked into more polarized, restricted patterns of thinking.

The question to ask is: "To what degree am I able to be (or, to what degree is the person we want to help able to be) a gray-area thinker and look at the different emotional realms of life, including dependency, nurturing, assertiveness, curiosity, aggression, vulnerability, fear, intimacy, empathy, and so forth?" We have to look at all the different emotional realms and see to what degree there is gray-area thinking, and even reflective thinking. Then we work to help the person broaden his range of experience and progress to higher levels of thinking in each of the realms, taking into account his individual processing differences.

Points to Remember

Some of the more severe personality disorders, like the paranoid personality or the schizoid personality, can border into unrealistic perceptions of the world, and individuals with these patterns require, often, long-term therapeutic relationships to effect a gradual change. Others, like those with mild depressive or obsessive personality patterns, may respond more quickly to either treatment or life experiences that offer the following ingredients (also key for more severe cases):

- Developing mastery of each of the stages of emotional development
- Broadening the person's range of emotional experience
- Strengthening the sensory and motor processing abilities that may be limited.

Chapter 12

Bipolar Disorders

Bipolar disorders, commonly called mood swings, have received a lot of visibility in recent years, but are perplexing problems, particularly when they occur in children. As with other disorders we've looked at, bipolar disorders tend to exist on a continuum. Everyone has some mood swings in the normal range, and many individuals have moderate mood swings that are never treated and are just an aspect of their cycle of life that they get used to. They have periods of productivity and high energy and euphoria and other periods of being low and down. These periods may last weeks, days, hours, or they may last months at a time.

Other individuals, however, are more extreme in their mood swings. They can be very high and agitated, talk rapidly, and have irrational, grand thoughts; later, they can be very depressed and gloomy and have equally intense, irrational thoughts about how awful life is and how terrible they are and how it may not even be worthwhile existing on the earth. So, with the highs can come agitation, as well as rapid speech and fragmented thinking; with the lows can come agitation, too, sometimes, but also lethargy, self-absorption, hopelessness, helplessness, and feelings of worthlessness.

In children with these patterns, we tend to see more impulsivity and agitation during the highs; during the low periods, the child's actions may suggest a feeling that he doesn't even deserve to live, or sometimes he has thoughts about how life is not worth living or that he doesn't deserve to be part of the family. Often the child with bipolar patterns, particularly when in a high or agitated state, can alienate himself from the family. When he is impulsive or agitated, he may inadvertently be destructive or hurt a younger sibling, and parents may punish and blame him in a way that just reinforces his sense of guilt and fuels the downward part of the cycle. Then, in his low period, he has all the evidence he needs that he's not worthwhile because he's causing problems in the family. If the child's behavior is not properly understood as part of a bipolar pattern, family members can inadvertently make things worse, rather than helping the child regroup and recover. The child's chronic states of impulsivity and agitation can lead him to being identified as the bad apple in the family, which either fuels his agitation because he wants to deny it, or fuels his gloomy and low periods because he believes it.

Similar situations happen with bipolar adults. In their high periods they can make mistakes, such as poor investments with family money or going on buying sprees, and then they may get a lot of criticism from spouses, friends, or family members, which only increases the depressive or gloomy part of the cycle. So it's very important to understand the dynamics of the syndrome.

The Biology of Bipolar Disorders

While bipolar patterns are thought to be fueled by biological differences, psychological factors play a role in triggering episodes and in intensifying mood swings. However, let's begin by looking at some of the physical differences that we've found to be part of the developmental pathway associated with this disorder, based on our clinical observations of both children and adults. Then we can look at the developmental pathway involved to help us determine the best course of action to help people with this disorder improve.

In my clinical experience, I have found that individuals with bipolar tendencies have a very unusual pattern of sensory processing and motor planning. As a group, they tend to be extremely over-reactive to sensation (although there are always individual variations and exceptions to the rule) from early on in life. Picture an infant or toddler who's hyper-responsive to sound, touch, emotional expressions, and the like. At the same time, when he gets overloaded, in part, due to the hyper-responsiveness, because there's too much touching or commotion or too many bright lights or too much emotion in the family, he does not become cautious and retreat as the hyper-responsive, fearful child does, or become negative and stubborn, as other hyper-responsive children might be to cope with the overload. The child prone to bipolar patterns tends to go into an action mode and seek out sensation.

So the child gets agitated, he moves around, and he's into everyone else's business. What turns the switch from hyper-responsiveness to craving sensation is often the experience of overload. Typically, the preschooler or toddler gets overloaded and then, rather than getting cautious or negative, which he might be some of the time, instead turns on and becomes very active, agitated, impulsive, and interfering. He may beat up on a younger sibling or pester an older sibling or get aggressive with parents. He may yell and scream or use foul language. In doing so, he actually overloads his sensory processing system even more, and then gets even more agitated or impulsive.

Even with older children, adolescents, and adults we see some of those patterns. There is a cycle in which the person, trying to cope with his overload, instead digs the hole deeper. Instead of retreating so he can quiet down and regulate himself, he increases his dysregulation. So, it's up to the person's family, friends, co-workers, teachers, and/or therapists to try to offset that tendency and calm the environment down. This can be a problem in therapy sessions, if the therapist doesn't understand these patterns and becomes confrontational and intrusive instead of being soothing and regulating. Others in the person's environment may also have this unhelpful tendency. In response, the person just gets more argumentative, agitated, grandiose, or impulsive.

It's this unique pattern of over-reactivity to sensation coupled with the craving for sensation that really characterizes the sensory processing and physical aspects of bipolar disorders. In addition, however, many people with bipolar disorders tend to have challenges in their motor planning and sequencing abilities, so they don't have a very organized sense of how their bodies work. Many are a little weaker on the visual-spatial processing side—their big-picture thinking—than they are on the verbal side, where many may be quite gifted, although some may have auditory and language processing problems, too. So, the typical picture is of an individual who gets overloaded and then craves sensation and can't rely on his organization of the body or sense of the big picture to re-organize himself. He is good at focusing on details, though, and may have a good verbal ability, at least for details. He may become more and more verbal as he gets more and more agitated.

However, we do also see bipolar patterns in individuals who have language problems, and in some children with autistic spectrum disorders. This disorder can be part of other disorders or mental illnesses, as well. There's a diagnosis of a thought disorder called schizo-affected disorder, in which the individual may have unrealistic thoughts about people chasing him or following him, for example, and also tends to have bipolar mood swings. In recent years there's been a tendency to see this whole pattern as part of a bipolar pattern rather than a combination of a thought disorder and a bipolar pattern.

There are psychological features to the developmental pathway, but these physical features are quite distinct and unusual; according to our clinical observations, it seems that in all likelihood the genetic or constitutional maturational differences that many clinicians and researchers have observed to be at the foundation of bipolar disorders express themselves not as a direct link from a genetic pattern into bipolar mood swings, but through this particular, unique sensory processing pattern.

Psychological Characteristics of Bipolar Patterns

To address the interpersonal or psychological characteristics of bipolar disorders, let's look again at our picture of a toddler, with this tendency to get overloaded and then swing into a pattern or craving sensation. Picture a caregiver who soothes the child when the child begins to get agitated, who counter-regulates and helps the child calm down immediately, like saying, "Oh, my little sweetheart is getting so excited—let's calm down." The caregiver then reduces the lights, lays a soft blanket over the child, talks in a softer tone, slows down the pace, and doesn't respond to the provocation with anger. Instead she tries to shift to an activity, maybe involving music or rhythmic movement, which is calming for the child. The key is that the rhythm of the interaction immediately switches from an agitated one to a calmer one.

When the same child is more self-absorbed, seems depressed, or in a low mood, the caregiver also counter-regulates, but this time by being energetic and helping the child energize up. The pace of the caregiver's voice, facial gestures, and emotional expressivity all increase. Also, the caregiver finds activities that the child likes and that build on his natural interests. If the child is interested in cars, or interested in a stuffed animal, the caregiver may say, "Oh, let's see what Mr. Bear is doing today!" or "Where does this little racecar want to go?" The goal is to help the child get reinvested and feel some energy and some positive value. The same basic process works when dealing with older children or adults. There's no phony praise to try to cheer someone up, but sincere engagement in the person's interests and a nice rhythm of interaction around those interests.

The key is in the rhythm of the interaction—the back-and-forth—and in always counter-regulating: soothe during agitation and energize up during low periods. This is true whatever the age or verbal abilities of the individual. Also, starting as soon as the small child becomes verbal, and even in the pre-verbal stage using gestures, the person with bipolar patterns needs to express the full range of feelings verbally and symbolically, not just through emotional expression. Whether he's experiencing anger, joy, sadness, hope, vulnerability, excitement, loss, assertiveness, curiosity, or humor, we want to encourage the individual to express the full range of human feeling gesturally and verbally. So in pretend play with the preschooler, conversations about school with the eight-year-old, or heart-to-heart talks between spouses, we want to help the person with bipolar disorder to elaborate all the feelings of life through lots of empathetic resonance.

We all have trouble dealing with certain feelings, so it can be hard to encourage the expression of those feelings in others. We may not want to listen to expressions of vulnerability, loss, sorrow, anger, or grandiosity because it hits too close to home, so we can find ourselves putting a stop to the expression of certain feelings. The thing to remember is that talking about feelings is different from acting them out. An adult or child who's talking about how angry she is and what she'd like to do to someone is not actually doing it. In fact, there's an inverse relationship, if you can talk about it or play it out in pretend, you're less likely to do it.

The only exception to this principle is when the individual is so preoccupied with only one theme that there's no balance or range. Say the child is constantly playing out aggression and anger and destructiveness in pretend play—there are always monsters attacking people or battles in which everyone dies. You can challenge the child to broaden the theme by bringing in doctors to help the injured people, for example. At the same time, you can explore the reasons for the anger, so you understand the deeper sources of it. Just watching as the child bangs dolls against the wall repetitively is not the same as broadening the drama of the pretend play and then having a discussion about why the child feels so angry.

The same thing holds in a conversation with an adult—we want to deepen the discussion. So, where there is a preoccupation with only one feeling, go deeper into the feeling, the reasons for it, the causes of it, the basis of it. Don't invalidate it—broaden it. Maybe there's hurt, there's pain, there's sorrow. There may be a sense of vulnerability behind it, so the deeper exploration broadens, often, the feeling's base. It can be hard to encourage expressions of vulnerability or humiliation or loss, because no one likes to talk about those feelings. And individuals with bipolar patterns often shy away from facing that vulnerable core or their neediness or their sense of loss. Even when someone with bipolar disorder is depressed, he feels like a bad person undeserving of help, rather than somebody who deserves to get help and can express his neediness. Feelings of humiliation are particularly difficult to express and often lead to violent behavior. No one is comfortable with feeling humiliated or ashamed or embarrassed.

As with the disorders discussed earlier, another component of helping someone to overcome bipolar disorders, or helping to prevent the manifestation of these disorders, is to help him move up the developmental ladder in the expression of feelings. We can help him to go from expressing them to looking at their causes, to comparing feelings, looking at the degrees of the feelings, doing gray-area thinking ("How angry, sad, or humiliated am I?"). Finally, we can help him to be reflective about the feeling, looking at how this feeling relate to the events that seem to lead to it. The mature individual can say, "Gee, the teacher only gave me a funny look and I'm feeling so depressed and down today. I think I'm over-reacting, but I don't know why and I'm curious about it."

It's important to encourage that degree of reflection, whether in a teenager or older child or in a 65-year-old adult. The older we are, the better our reflective ability and the broader the context. We can reflect back on a longer period of life and say, "I've always felt this way, since I was a child. Will this be permanent? Can I expect tomorrow to be better? Is there anything I can do to feel better?" These kinds of questions are aspects of the reflective thinking abilities that get stronger as we get older and negotiate the stages of emotional thinking.

It is also very important to help individuals with bipolar disorder to master their own environments, to know what their trigger points are and what kind of environment overloads them so they can try to regulate themselves. This process should start early in life. Parents, teachers, and other caregivers can help children to become more aware and begin to manage their interaction with the environment. Adults can learn to observe themselves feeling agitated in a situation, whether it's a busy party or a fractious debate with a spouse or colleague. They can use their reflective ability to say, "Oops, I'm getting agitated; I'd better slow down and maybe focus on something else." They can learn when they should take a time out, so to speak.

Under the framework of managing their interaction with the environment, we also want to include how people with bipolar disorders treat their bodies. For example, lots of caffeine or sugar can cause the body to rev up and become overloaded, so it's very important to be moderate with caffeine or sugar intake. There can be a tendency to get anxious, to feel bad, and then try to pick oneself up with lots of caffeine, sugar, herbal stimulants, or energy foods, and then these nutritional patterns can agitate one more and more. Other natural foods and remedies can be more soothing. The same principle applies with physical activities. For example, competitive sports can agitate, yoga can calm. So individuals with bipolar disorder have to take a balanced approach to the body, and, if they are very sensitive to certain food groups, they should avoid them or else have them very sparingly.

In other words, self-awareness and the ability to be reflective involve one's total environment. Addressing these different factors can help individuals who experience bipolar patterns, or even have been diagnosed with a disorder to help themselves or be helped by their close family members and colleagues.

Relationships that Intensify Bipolar Patterns

In contrast, other factors can exacerbate bipolar patterns and lead to greater chronicity of the disorder. If a young child has a caregiver who gets agitated along with the child, who gets more punitive, instead of setting calm, firm limits, and who revs the child up with yelling or harsh language or intrusive types of punishments, this intensifies both extremes of the pattern. Instead of helping the child identify feelings through pretend play and encouraging expression, the caregiver might cut off lines of communication around feelings with a firm "Children should be seen and not heard" kind of attitude. The family could be very formal and rigid, or very punitive, or could vacillate between overindulgence and punitiveness. Maybe there's a split where one parent is punitive and the other is overly indulgent. Any of these patterns makes a burgeoning bipolar pattern more pronounced and chronic.

Adults may have spouses or family members who have little tolerance for expressions of affect; they may not be empathetic and can't help the person empathize with himself. Instead of encouraging the person to move up the developmental ladder to gray-area and reflective thinking (gray-area thinking is by definition the opposite of bipolar thinking), they inadvertently cause polarized thinking by getting into all-or-nothing power struggles with the individual. The spouse or family member or may be an all-or-nothing person himself or herself, and the individual with bipolar disorder gets locked into these bipolar patterns more and more.

Creating a Comprehensive Program

It is particularly challenging to create a comprehensive program for individuals with bipolar patterns. The key is to create an environment that facilitates the healthy coping strategies and reduces any negative patterns. A treatment program often involves therapy (possibly as often as three times a week, but at least once a week), addressing the family patterns described above, and providing support for family members. It may also involve medication, particularly for adults. Children usually don't require medication, but they sometimes do. We like to recommend that children have a comprehensive program involving family work; if medication is considered, it should be part of an overall program.

Case Study of an Adult with Bipolar Disorder

A man in his late 20s—a distinguished trial attorney who we'll call Roger—had been extremely hypersensitive to touch and sound since childhood. His sensitivity helped him to be very attuned to others and he had good interpersonal skills. This helped him with his work; he was great at networking and could read juries very well. Fitting the pattern described above, he also was action-oriented and craved sensation. He liked skiing, driving fast, and he stayed up late at night. He was unmarried, was something of a womanizer, and he liked to drink and to experiment with different kinds of substances, not all legal, particularly stimulants.

Growing up, Roger had a very indulgent mother, but a very punitive father; neither one provided regulation or appropriate counter-balancing to their son's moods. His parents described him, in a rare extended family therapy session when Roger came to us, as a "moody, but brilliant child." As a child, Roger tended to be temperamental and have tantrums. He could get down very easily and could also get very excitable and demanding about new things he wanted to do. He would get into trouble at school by behaving impulsively, often getting overloaded by the sights and sounds and commotion, which led him to push or shove or beat up on another child. He was also prone to do that with his sister, so he was constantly in trouble with his father, who took a very hard, "law and order" approach, which frightened young Roger.

Roger's parents also said that his teachers had described him as moody, but they overlooked it because of his strong academic skills. He had a wonderful memory, particularly for words, and was an early reader. They saw him as a "special, though difficult, child." He had friends in grade school and in high school, but was prone to mood swings, and if a girlfriend disappointed him he would get deeply despondent. He would get very excited about each new project and would spend impulsively on some new article of clothing or gadget. He was into the latest in computers and would overspend when his parents let him. He had the same patterns of impulsivity coupled with strong academic performance in college and at a top law school.

Now, working as a lawyer, Roger was doing well at a firm, but was showing the same pattern of getting into trouble because of being hot-tempered and occasionally not following through with work commitments when he was depressed or despondent. He had tried therapy briefly but had managed, he said, "to seduce his therapist into being part of his fan club." He got the therapist to admire his skills, but he was not really helped through his challenges. He had begun to get in trouble with the law because he was arrested for speeding and drinking, and then got into arguments with the police. Roger's lawyer insisted on getting a more complete evaluation, which brought him to us.

We observed a man who, when we got him quiet and regulated and organized, could slow down and speak coherently. Otherwise he would talk a mile a minute, bragging about his latest feat in court or the latest gadget he'd bought, and he expressed very little reflection over his emotional tendencies, and showed poor judgment and all-or-nothing thinking. In the office, he demonstrated being easily overloaded and hyper-aware of any kind of extraneous sound or sight. His fine motor coordination, when he had to write things, was sluggish and weak. Also, he was more of a "tree" person—good with details and subtleties, but lacking the "big picture" and showing poor visual-spatial skills. For example, he found it hard to find the office; he went around to all the wrong doors, even though there were good instructions as to the right door into the office.

Roger had not been on medication yet because his former therapist thought his problems could be handled just with therapy and insight, but Roger hadn't really been treated with a developmental approach. During the evaluation phase, before we got a program started, he went out one evening and took a lot of substances with stimulant qualities. He briefly lost his sense of reality testing and had to go into a hospital for a few days in a kind of frenzy of activity and stream-of-consciousness, rapid speaking, and illogical thought. It wasn't clear whether he was actually delusional, in the sense of believing in an irrational system at this time, but he was talking about his special power to get any criminal off anywhere in the world just with his glib tongue.

When we saw Roger after he settled down (having been given major tranquilizers to calm him down), we began outlining a comprehensive approach. It involved intensive psychotherapy with a therapist trained in this developmental approach, someone who understood Roger's sensory system and could offer counter-regulation and soothing when Roger was hyper, as well as a lot of energizing up when he was depressed and despondent. Another of the therapist's goals was to help Roger understand his needs for counter-regulating environments and relationships. We also got Roger involved with an occupational therapist who works with adults on a series of self-calming techniques and what we call sensory-regulating techniques to help him learn to regulate his hyper-sensitivity and also to develop constructive outlets for his craving for sensation. Roger was very musical, so music provided one pattern of a rhythmic outlet. There were also certain sports he liked, which were utilized to help regulate his need for sensation. We did rhythmic exercises with him—varying speeds and patterns as part of fun activities—just like we would with a child, to help Roger learn to regulate himself.

Roger's therapist helped him move from polarized thinking to gray-area, more subtle thinking, always counter-regulating to help him maintain longer sequences of affective interaction. The goal was for Roger to develop gray-area thinking at the pre-verbal level—functioning not just in extremes of mood, but also in the middle ranges with more subtle back-and-forth communication—as well as at the verbal level. So, for example, when Roger would get a little hyper the therapist would soothingly ask him to describe what was going on, which helped him modulate his mood a little bit and get into more of a gray-area pattern, rather than jumping between a hyper pattern and a despondent pattern. The therapist also helped him describe the subtle nuances of his feelings.

Working with the therapist, over a period of about a year Roger began to master gray-area thinking, and then after about another year he became more reflective and able to describe his own feelings vis-à-vis what he thought he felt or ought to feel or what other people might feel in a similar situation. So he began to measure his response, given the facts of a situation, and could identify patterns and say things like, "This situation is making me more upset than I probably ought to be; I must have overly high expectations and not take disappointment very well." The therapist also worked with Roger on accepting feelings of disappointment, frustration, and humiliation, because these are the feelings he ran away from and that would also trigger his pattern of craving sensation and grandiose thinking.

There was less of a focus on working with Roger's family dynamics, although these dynamics contributed to his challenges, because it wasn't expected that simple awareness of the patterns would lead to significantly corrective changes. The therapist did help Roger come to some insights, through discussion, about how he had developed his patterns. He realized how having a punitive father and an indulgent mother had facilitated his dysregulation and contributed to some of the feelings he had growing up, such as his fear of his father, his feeling of being over-invested in by his mother, and how the sense of competition his father engendered in him had scared him and led to his developing a false sense of bravado early in life, which further supported his craving for sensation.

While Roger addressed these patterns with his primary therapist, he was also working with a skillful occupational therapist. (In some cases, working with someone who understands the how the sensory and motor systems work is sufficient; a trained occupational therapist is not always necessary.) The program also included working with a visual-spatial specialist who followed the work of Harry Wachs and his book, *Thinking Goes to School*, to strengthen Roger's visual-spatial skills—his ability to be a big-picture and reflective thinker with visual material—so his sense of direction and body awareness improved. We also worked on Roger's coordination and motor planning skills to improve his sequencing and help him to get more security in his body.

Finally, because Roger's lifestyle involved lots of drinking and experimental substances, we had him see a psycho-pharmacologist for medication. He was put on mood stabilizers, which helped him to maintain a more consistent pattern in the short term and to participate in a comprehensive program. Fortunately, he was very motivated to improve; he realized how much was at stake in terms of his career. The law enforcement agencies had let him off with a stern warning, provided he get involved in a comprehensive program.

In the five years since beginning the program (which is ongoing), Roger made very, very consistent progress. By the third year, he had developed sufficient reflective abilities to sustain himself and his progress without medication, although we continue to hold medication in reserve, as needed, mindful that stress or other life events could trigger regression. He's now in a more consistent relationship with a young woman that may lead to marriage and family life. While he's still highly energetic and prone to periodic polarized thinking, he has better relationships and is clearly on the road toward a more even mood and more gray-area and reflective thinking about his emotional life.

Case Study of a Child with Bipolar Patterns

An eight-year-old boy, whom we'll call Justin, had a very similar pattern to Roger's. Justin demonstrated polarized thinking, lack of mood regulation, and despondency, though he didn't yet show grandiose thinking or substance abuse. He wasn't in a real depression, but he had the depressed ideation that he was bad, and he sometimes wanted to jump out of a window. The family dynamics were also similar to Roger's, but in Justin's case, his mother was the punitive one and his father was more indulgent. He didn't get the modulation that he needed and, when his mother got angry at him for harassing and beating up his younger brother, Justin would go from being agitated to depressed.

We instituted a comprehensive program for Justin like the one we created for Roger, only without medication because we had caught Justin's disorder at a much earlier age and we weren't dealing with acute challenges yet. Justin is now in his early teen years, and we have been seeing consistent progress and a shift toward gray-area and reflective thinking.

Points to Remember

To help an individual with a bipolar disorder, we need to develop a comprehensive program that includes the following components:

- Counter-regulating interactions that calm the individual when he is over-stimulated, and energize him up when he is depressed
- Encouraging the expression of the *full* range of feelings, verbally and gesturally, including deepening and broadening themes on which the person may be on is fixated to the exclusion of other themes
- Helping the person move up the developmental ladder in terms of levels of thinking, especially thinking about feelings
- Teaching the person to manage his interactions with the environment, including taking care of his body by nutrition and exercise choices that are regulating
- Using medication when necessary, as an adjunct to the other elements of a comprehensive program.

Chapter 13

Addictive Behaviors and Substance Abuse

People can be addicted to a wide range of substances and activities—food, illegal drugs, legal drugs, gambling, and so forth. There is a panoply of addictive behaviors and substance abuse. However, although each type of problem has its own unique profile for each individual, all of these challenges share some common features and common developmental pathways. This allows us to formulate an approach that individuals and families can take to begin overcoming addictions, whatever their nature.

Developmental Pathways Toward Addictive Behaviors

Sensory Processing Profiles

For various addictive behaviors such as alcoholism and substance abuse, there has been a lot of research suggesting genetic or familial components, though this hasn't been nailed down to any specific gene. Many physical and neurological illnesses are the product of a gene or a group of genes, but that is not the case for mental health disorders. The most we can say at this point is that there may be a variety of genetic factors and patterns involved, and different individuals and families may have different combinations of these factors or patterns. This research is ongoing and we anticipate new insights in the years to come.

What we do know more about, however, are what we call constitutional maturational differences, in other words, physical differences that may have genetic, intrauterine, and/or early experiential origins. Some of these experiences may involve exposure to toxic substances—*in utero* or early in development—that affect the physical structure of the nervous system. Certain types of familial interactions and stresses can affect the structure of the nervous system as well. So, there are physical differences and there are a number of factors that can affect these differences. For example, many years ago, while studying multi-risk families, we found that babies who were born with very good sensory modulation would, within one month, become very over-reactive to sensation due to their chaotic home environments. This characteristic stayed with them for many years, making them similar to babies who were born with sensory modulation challenges that resulted from intrauterine or genetic factors.

One subgroup of people with addictive tendencies is hyper-responsive to sensation. People in this subgroup use addictive behaviors to calm themselves down, especially as they get older. They might use legal or illegal substances or food (or certain types of food) to self-regulate. People who drink large amounts of coffee or who smoke a lot may be using the substance in a self-calming way—to increase focus or solve problems—even though caffeine and nicotine are stimulants.

Other individuals, however, crave sensation, and the substances or behaviors to which they become addicted are a way to fulfill that need for sensation—it is a way to increase sensory arousal. The person who craves sensation and is always taking risks to "rev up their nervous system," as one risk-taker described it, is an example of that phenomenon.

And then some people are under-reactive and self-absorbed, and because they have come to relate to the world in that way, they may elect to use substances (illegal and quasi-legal) that increase their inner-directed state of mind, increase their fantasy life, and increase their removal from outer reality.

Lower Levels of Emotional Development and Thinking

A person with addictive tendencies may have any one of a variety of sensory processing profiles. However, there is a common feature of addictive behavior, which is that, once under the influence of the addictive pattern—whether it relates to a particular substance such as alcohol or a specific activity such as gambling—the individual does not show age-expected capacities for social and emotional development or reflective thinking. They are not able to say, for example, "If I keep smoking at the rate I'm going, it will probably affect my health, so it's time for me to stop," and then follow through on that decision.

Even for individuals who may be brilliant in their careers—they may be professors of philosophy or successful in business, and have good reflective thinking when it comes to comparing two philosophies or two business strategies—their feelings around the addictive behavior tend to cluster around two lower levels of thinking: the polarized (all-or-nothing) level of logical thinking, and pre-logical or fragmented thinking (also called "magical thinking"). So, around the addiction, the individual does not use a great deal of reflective thinking about long-term consequences. He says, "I've got to have a drink NOW!" He does not say, "I'm upset and really want a drink, but if I have one, then I'll just want more and that's going to make my problems worse, not better, so I won't have one." He has unrealistic ideas, believing that the substance or activity makes him more powerful, brilliant, and creative.

The person may also get stuck in an even earlier stage of thinking, in which he doesn't use ideas at all; he just translates an impulse or intent into an impulsive behavior. Whether it's the addictive behavior itself, such as gambling or taking drugs, or the behavior that supports the addiction, such as stealing to support a drug habit, there's an urge and then an action, rather than an *idea* which would allow the person to think about the urge or discuss it with others in a flexible way, or fantasize about it and achieve some mastery over the urge through fantasy. Instead, it gets translated right away into impulsive action: grabbing someone's wallet to get money to buy drugs.

People with addictive patterns may show higher levels of social and emotional development and thinking in other areas of their lives such as the way they relate to their spouses and children and the way they conduct themselves at work if they keep the addictive behavior circumscribed. But there is a tendency, obviously, for the behavior to permeate more and more of the person's life, and so more areas become characterized by these earlier developmental levels. At some point it goes from being an encapsulated segment of an otherwise healthy life to a pervasive pattern.

This process happens to varying degrees, depending on the individual. Some people may have many, many years in which the earlier developmental levels characterize just narrow sectors of their lives. From our clinical experience, however, we would say that the lion's share of people who are prone to addictive behavior tend to have trouble maintaining age-expected thinking and social and emotional coping abilities at the higher levels of thinking in many areas of their lives. The addictive behaviors are the more striking examples of this, and characterize the lowest levels of functioning, but other areas are not usually working as well as we'd want them to either. Therefore, people with addictive tendencies can benefit from work that helps them advance in all areas.

Family Patterns

People with addictive tendencies often have family histories in which the ability to use emotional signaling rather than action to cope with frustration or challenge was not adequately developed. We see, even at the toddler stage, less emotional interaction and less joint regulation between caregiver and child. Then the child becomes more vulnerable to impulsive actions or to being a little bit withdrawn. Because of that vulnerability, at each subsequent level of development, the use of ideas is not solidified. There certainly may be the capacity for imaginative play and using ideas, but it is not as rich as would be typical, and it doesn't cover the full range of emotions. There is constriction in the realm of frustration and disappointment, in particular.

There are also constrictions when the person moves forward to the level of connecting ideas together and logical thinking, and then again at the stages of multi-causal thinking, gray- area thinking, and then finally reflective thinking. As in the earlier stages, the feelings that typically don't get incorporated into the advanced levels of reflective thinking are those having to do with loss, disappointment, frustration, anger, and, often, dependency. Addictive behaviors and substance abuse then can serve as a substitute for advanced problem-solving and reflection when it comes to dealing with these feelings.

A Program for Overcoming Addictions and Addictive Behaviors

A program that can help individuals with addictions should involve a number of elements in a comprehensive, orchestrated manner. First, it is important to focus on the physical aspects. We want to help the person to become better regulated, and also to wean themselves off the addiction itself, because if it is food or another substance that is ingested, there is often a physiological addiction that has built up (even to foods and substances that are not addictive by nature). It can take a couple of weeks before the yearnings or cravings go away, and if it's a drug, it may take longer than that.

Additionally, individuals who are addicted to drugs that hype up their nervous system tend also to eat a lot of foods that hype up the nervous system as well. Therefore, it's important for the person to begin a very healthy diet of vegetables, fruits, complex grains, and organic meat and fish so they aren't affected by any chemicals, artificial preservatives, additives, food coloring, dyes, or anything that converts to sugar very quickly in the body (which will change moods and regulatory patterns). Some people may have specific allergies or sensitivities to foods such as wheat products, dairy products, or corn, so that should be checked out.

In addition to a regulating nutritional plan, individuals who are under-reactive, over-reactive, or who crave sensation all benefit enormously from regular exercise programs geared to their particular sensory pattern. There should be daily workouts that are both fun and regulating. The key is that the person feels good and organized afterwards.

Once this baseline program is established, then we want to help the person develop relationships with a lot of back-and-forth emotional cueing and support, particularly around feelings of frustration, disappointment, and loss. We want to have lots of emotional gesturing and signaling around these feeling states in particular, and then we want to move up through the developmental stages: exchanging ideas, thinking logically, thinking reflectively by looking at the causes and reasons for feelings, and looking at feelings from multiple angles and in shades of gray. We can help the person develop more judgment and reflection by playing the "Thinking About Tomorrow" game described earlier. The person anticipates situations that may come up and how he'll feel about them, how others involved may feel, how he typically deals with these sorts of situations, and alternative ways he could deal with the situation the next time.

Many people need intensive psychotherapy to strengthen healthy patterns, and the therapist can orchestrate the whole therapeutic program, working with the family as well (either the person's spouse and children or his family of origin, if it is a child, teenager, or adult who is still living with his parents). Sometimes, residential care is needed at first for detoxifying from an addictive substance, or weaning off the addictive behavior and establishing healthy physical patterns and the beginning of the therapeutic process.

The key is to continue the therapeutic program after the residential or inpatient component. Frequently, individuals battling addictions can do very well during the residential phase because they have a lot of support, nurturance, and structure, but then once they're out on their own, they relapse. They need an adequate post-residential or post-hospital plan with structure and limits, as well as the other components discussed above. It may have to be very intensive, with strong limits—monitoring urine and blood, for example—under the assumption that the person will regress to impulsive or illogical thought patterns or polarized thinking when the yearnings get strong again, even if they are over the physiologic addiction.

Even with an intensive therapeutic program with lots of checks and balances, relapses can be expected. There are be ups and downs, and the first residential treatment program may not work permanently. But the overall pattern should be one of gradual progress, as long as we have created an environment that supports the higher levels of thinking while also setting firm limits and benchmarks, recognizing that the individual has a lifelong vulnerability.

It's especially important to keep up the diet and exercise components that create a firm physical foundation for progress. Interestingly, the first sign, sometimes, of regression is that the person changes his physical patterns of exercise and nutrition. For example, if the person has a wheat or grain allergy, then starting to eat bread again can make him yearn for alcohol made from grains. So if that is part of the person's pattern, staying away from grains is very, very important. Knowing the person's physical profile is crucial for everyone involved.

Case Study of an Adult with Addictions

To illustrate the treatment of addictions, let's look at the case of Dan. At 32, Dan had a sensory-craving profile; he was a gambler, a womanizer, and liked to take risks such as skydiving. While running around with friends, Robert began experimenting with illegal stimulants. The drugs gave him a sense of power and well-being, and allowed him to stay up all night. He often mixed the stimulants with alcohol. He had already been prone to impulsivity and somewhat polarized thinking. As he got more and more involved in substance abuse, his risk-taking and illogical thought patterns increased, until he finally got into hot water with the law.

Robert's family and friends finally brought him to a hospital, where he was able to get off the illegal drugs through a combination of tranquilizers, mood stabilizers, and also some anti-depressants, because he got very depressed once he began coming down. However, he was released quickly without a very good after-care pattern; a therapist was assigned to him for follow-up but Robert stopped going to therapy after three weeks. He was all right for several months, and then regressed and went through this pattern again. He had three hospitalizations, all repeating the same pattern. Finally his family, along with a new therapist who evaluated him, realized that Robert really needed residential care for three to five months to get more fully involved in the therapeutic process, and he needed a much more intensive after-care program.

The program, with all the elements described above, including daily therapy, was implemented. Ten years later, Robert is married and has a few children. He is doing well, but he still has therapy three times a week and has his urine and blood checked periodically for illegal substances. He realizes he has a chronic, long-term vulnerability, and still talks about craving the "highs" of the days when he did drugs. However, he recognizes that those feelings led him to a place to which he doesn't want to return.

The subject of addictions is not simple. There are many different varieties of addictions and addictive behaviors. When the problem seems minor, such addictions to certain foods, or occasional gambling binges, then the therapeutic intervention may be less intensive. When it's a major league substance addiction, then there is the double whammy of the addictive disorder plus the effect of the substance addiction itself that must be addressed with much more intensive treatment. In either case, there's no substitute for a comprehensive program that addresses all the levels of addictive tendencies. The ultimate goal is to help the individual become a reflective thinker in all areas of life, including, and particularly, in the area of what was the addictive pattern, which means that the person can evaluate himself and take corrective action on his own. That's the signal that he is progressing well, though even then therapy should continue to monitor, maintain, and reinforce that.

Points to Remember

A comprehensive program to help those with addictive behavior and substance abuse challenges should address all the levels of addictive tendencies through the following steps:

- Wean the person from the physiological addiction, if relevant, and address physical regulation through nutrition, exercise, and so forth.
- Build relationships with a lot of back-and-forth emotional signaling around difficult feeling states such as frustration, disappointment, and loss.
- Help the person move up through the developmental stages to reflective thinking.
- Include intensive psychotherapy as needed to help the person recover, and to oversee long-term progress and address relapses and regression.

Chapter 14

The Effects of Trauma

Trauma takes many forms. In the broadest sense, we can define it as an extremely frightening, even terrifying, emotionally overwhelming experience. Trauma can result from group or community events: wars, natural disasters such as hurricanes and earthquakes, and incidents such as terrorist attacks and school shootings. It can also result from personal events—the loss of a loved one, an assault, being robbed, or even the loss of abilities through the aging process. The common denominator, however, is the experience of overwhelming negative feelings and the various reactions to these feelings. Whatever the cause of trauma, there are ways we can help others, whether they're children, adults, or the elderly, to cope with these overwhelming experiences.

First and foremost we should recognize that the signs of trauma, like the causes of trauma, can take many forms. Beginning in early infancy, each of us has a different way of demonstrating that we're feeling overwhelmed, frightened, angry, hopeless, and/or helpless, or a combination of these emotions. Some children withdraw; it's not unusual for a 14-month-old who's lost caregivers, even just for a short time because of a business trip, to become more withdrawn and self-absorbed. A child's response to trauma can manifest as anxiety, nightmares, obsessive fears, and depression, as well as anger. Older children, often, become aggressive and want to hurt others in response to a frightening experience or set of experiences. A response to trauma can involve inflicting the same kind of trauma on others; victims of sexual abuse often become abusers themselves. It can involve impulsive behavior, such as setting fires or the like.

The form a child's reaction takes depends on his own unique history and his physical disposition. One child who is active and craves sensation may become more agitated, active, and aggressive after a traumatic experience. Another child who's more laid-back and tends to sleep a lot may become self-absorbed and withdraw into his own fantasy life. Adults, too, manifest different reactions to trauma. Anxiety, depression, impulsivity, alcoholism, gambling problems, aggression, and delinquent behavior can all be responses to traumatic events. In addition, recent studies have shown that individuals exposed to four or more traumatic events in early childhood were *one- to four-thousand-fold* more likely to have medical problems—such as obesity, alcoholism, and pulmonary problems—as adults than people with fewer or no traumatic experiences. Thus, the effects of trauma can continue throughout life, without proper treatment.

To help traumatized individuals, we first need to determine the particular form of the person's response to trauma. Then, we assess to what degree the response is disrupting healthy development or healthy functioning. In other words, some adults may experience nightmares and occasional anxiety attacks, but they can continue to work and to be loving parents. With others, however, the effects of trauma may be more pervasive. We may see severe depression, which interrupts work and family life because the individual sleeps all day or is overwhelmed, perhaps, by feelings of despair and even thoughts of suicide. So, we need to ask, to what degree does the effect of trauma disrupt the person's ability to think, reason, and plan? To what degree does it disrupt relationships at work and at home? To what degree does it disrupt the person's basic ability to interact or regulate his moods?

With an understanding of how pervasive the effects of the trauma are, we can plan our intervention accordingly. Some people may require hospitalization or more comprehensive care; others, a more limited program. In either case, there are common principles that can help all individuals—from infants through the elderly—begin overcoming trauma and regaining healthy functioning. Before we outline these principles, we want to emphasize an important overarching concept, which is that the sooner we institute a program in relationship to the traumatic event, the more effective the program is likely to be. While it's always possible to help someone along the path of recovery, the earlier the trauma is addressed, the better. In this regard, looking at a frightening and almost incomprehensible event, such as a school shooting, we should really have trained people available on the spot to help, rather than playing catch-up later. Of course, in the case of a natural disaster such as a hurricane, it is necessary to reestablish vital services, but we also should deal with the emotional and social consequences of the trauma as quickly as possible.

Principles of Effective Intervention for Trauma

Restoring a Feeling of Security

The first and most important principle in helping someone who's been traumatized is to reestablish a feeling of security and safety. Whatever the nature of the traumatic event, the person feels unsafe, insecure, and very frightened, regardless of whether these feelings manifest through anxiety, depression, or behavior problems. It's vital, therefore, to reestablish a sense of safety and security.

In the case of a community trauma such as war or a natural disaster, we want to establish vital services—food, supplies, shelter, medical care—as quickly as possible, while providing the security of a team of caring, helpful people. Sometimes the local or international community does this reasonably well, though on occasion we get "caught with our pants down." We're not properly ready, don't coordinate services well, and don't restore a sense of security quickly enough. This ends up perpetuating the traumatic experience for many individuals. So we have to improve our ability to respond quickly and appropriately, addressing the psychological factors as well as the physical ones.

When the trauma is personal, for example, a toddler whose parent is dying, we need other adults to provide security and nurturing in a regular way so that the child feels safe. This sense of safety is paramount, even over other important considerations, once basic survival needs have been met. Sometimes children who are victims of sexual abuse may be interviewed by law enforcement officials too quickly to "get information." Even if it is done in a way that the officials feel is supportive, if a parent or other trusted adult isn't allowed in the room while the child is retelling the event to a stranger, the child only becomes more traumatized. It may be important to get information so that the culprit doesn't abuse others, but there's no reason not to do it in the presence of an adult who makes the child feel safe and secure. It also helps to have a skillful mental health professional there as part of the group that helps the child identify what happened and who did it. Reestablishing this sense of security is equally important for adults as well, of course.

Another mistake we often make is assuming that it's important for the person to re-tell the event, to unburden himself of the trauma, to play it out or talk it out. However, if we encourage or pressure the person to do that too quickly, the reliving of the event only re-frightens him. Of course, we shouldn't prevent or discourage the person from working through it. We should certainly create the opportunity for the young child to play out the event with symbolic toys and dolls, and give the adult comfortable opportunities to talk it out, but let the person do it at his own pace. Don't probe or intrude, otherwise we just compound the insecurity and trauma.

Reestablishing Engagement

The second principle is to reestablish engagement or relationship with the most trusted, nurturing, constant individual in the person's life. In some situations—in a refugee camp for people fleeing a war, for example—this may be difficult, but we should at least try to provide a nurturing relationship for children, even temporarily. In the case of a child whose parents are ill, a relative or close family friend—someone who will be part of that child's life for a long time—should come in and establish a trusting, nurturing relationship.

Adults or elderly people who are sick or have been injured and need to spend a long time in the hospital can also experience a loss of closeness. We want to have flexibility where a loved one can stay in the hospital room with the adult, just as we do with infants, on a cot or a bed. This relationship provides an ongoing, protective sense of warmth and security, which helps the person, of whatever age, regain trust in the world and believe that the world can be a safe and loving place, not just a frightening place. That's vital for overcoming the traumatic event and the overwhelming feelings the person has.

Encouraging Communication

Once the sense of security is established, and a nurturing relationship is in place, then we can focus on helping traumatized individuals communicate whatever they want to communicate. Even for someone who is verbal, the process might begin at the simplest gestural level: exchanging smiles, frowns, hand gestures, hugs or non-invasive touching. Individuals who are too traumatized to talk may be able to engage in nonverbal communication only around negotiating basic needs for food, going to the bathroom, and other basics of life. Children who aren't speaking need opportunities to play.

With children and adults who are able to talk, we should make opportunities for nonverbal and verbal communication in the context of the nurturing relationship described above, without probing. Let the person take the lead; he may want to know where the next meal is coming from, or need reassurance that bombs won't drop anymore. Perhaps he just needs talk about whatever is on his mind. Listening, empathizing, and encouraging people to talk about what they want to talk about (or communicate nonverbally, if that's all they can do) helps them to improve. Just reestablishing that they can communicate, they can control their environment through nonverbal and verbal communication, enhances that sense of safety and security and helps them regain a sense of trust in the world.

Telling the Story of the Traumatic Event

Once a sense of security, a nurturing relationship, and basic communication have been reestablished (this can take anywhere from days to weeks to months or even years), we want to help the person tell the story of the traumatic experience in his own words, in his own way. The goal is for him to explore his feelings—particularly the frightening and sad feelings—and his reactions to his feelings, especially reactions he may be ashamed of, such as anger or helplessness or guilt. But we don't lead the person or have preconceived notions about what his feelings should be. Each individual has his own reactions to trauma.

There may be positive feelings, too, such as relief at surviving or pride at helping someone else, in addition to feelings of profound loss and sadness and mourning for loved ones who were lost. It's very important to let the person tell her story in her own way, and then encourage her to broaden the story to address many different aspects of her emotions. This should occur over many months, in the context of a therapeutic relationship. Almost all individuals who have been exposed to trauma should have a relationship with a mental health professional skilled at helping people describe, cope with, and elaborate feelings.

Helping Others

Finally, it's very helpful for individuals coping with trauma and loss to do something that helps others—to take an active step and turn their passive and helpless experience into something constructive. This may be related to the particular trauma they suffered—raising funds for future victims of natural disasters or sending cards to children with cancer, for example—or not, as the person wants. Friends, family, and therapists can suggest possibilities, but we want the decision to be made by the individual. This can be done on a personal level, or in conjunction with an organization. It's a very important component of the healing process, but can only happen once the other aspects are in place.

The key in all these steps is trusting relationships—initially with family members or close friends, if possible, and then with a mental health professional or a team of professionals who can help mediate the process. Also, organizations that work with victims of trauma can create programs that incorporate these principles, and the principles should be supported by governmental agencies. Obviously, for many disasters and traumatic events one key is better prevention—identifying risk factors and taking action—this is an equally important aspect of handling trauma.

Secondary Trauma

Another phenomenon worth mentioning here is secondary trauma. This affects people who are not directly traumatized, but who have seen what's happened to another person and worry that it might happen to them, or maybe even feel guilty that it happened to someone else instead of them, and need to be reassured that there are preventive strategies in place. This reassurance is vital to establishing a sense of security for those suffering from secondary trauma. Beyond that, the principles for addressing secondary trauma are the same as those described above for trauma, but of course they're easier to implement and progress is much quicker, especially for children.

Case Studies of Trauma

A Child Affected by Trauma

Three-year-old Ruben lost his mother in a car accident just as he was beginning to talk in full sentences and think logically (for example, when asked a question like, "Why do you want to go outside?" he could answer, "Because I want to play"). For the first day or two after the accident, he knew something had happened to Mommy, but his father didn't tell him anything. Ruben's grandparents moved into the house with them, but Ruben wanted his Mommy, and started crying and started having terrible nightmares. Gradually they told him that Mommy had been in a car accident and had gone to heaven. Ruben alternately cried and looked very sad, and started saying things like, "I want to go to heaven to be with Mommy. What do I have to do to go to heaven?" He saw something on television about how people who die go to heaven, and he talked about jumping off the house so he could die and go to heaven with Mommy.

Obviously, Ruben's father and grandparents were very concerned. They tried to reassure him that they loved him and would always be there for him and that Mommy was with them in spirit, but none of this seemed to calm little Ruben down. When he was brought to us for a consultation, we saw that Ruben was maintaining his ability to be related, interactive, and verbal. He could engage in symbolic play and think logically, but he was very despondent and concerned about "being with Mommy." His reaction was one mostly of sadness and longing, not one of aggression or agitation; he also had a lot of fears about losing his father and grandparents.

We instituted a program that incorporated the four steps described above and asked Ruben's father to take off work for three weeks. It was time for his summer vacation and Ruben needed the security of Daddy being home. Because Ruben didn't know his grandparents very well (they had lived in another city), we asked if they could make a longer-term commitment to stay with Ruben. Fortunately, they had the flexibility to relocate, so they moved in more permanently, and—along with Daddy being home more—that gave Ruben the extra sense of security, nurturing, and consistency he needed, and his desire to join Mommy in heaven lessened. He began sharing the view that Mommy's spirit—her warmth and her feelings—was still in the house, even though he couldn't see her. He looked at pictures and old videos of her with his father and his grandparents. Even though doing this could have triggered more feelings of loss, it was something he wanted to do and something his father and grandparents wanted to do as well.

We also established a pattern of doing a lot of Floortime-type play to establish good communication patterns. Ruben played out issues indirectly with animals: some animals were dying, lions and tigers were angry and ate up other animals. It was clear he was coping with a lot of anger about Mommy not being there; he vacillated between themes of loss, themes of anger, and themes of fear in his play. We coached his father to empathize with and play out whatever theme Ruben chose—not to try to relate it to Mommy or to play shrink and interpretations. Twice a week Ruben's father brought him to therapy sessions, in which they basically did the same thing—they played out his feelings.

After about six weeks Ruben went back to his preschool program and got back into a routine. Thinking about Mommy and missing her and looking at her pictures became a part of his daily, and then weekly, routine, and he returned to a state of being sad, but not the overwhelming despondency he felt before. About a year later, Ruben thought that being able to look at a scrapbook with pictures of Mommy and mementoes of things they used to do together would be helpful. So, he and his father, who was actually quite a good artist, designed a web-based scrapbook that anyone could download and use to remember loved ones they had lost. In this way we incorporated the fifth step for dealing with trauma—helping others—into Ruben's healing process.

An Adult Affected by Trauma

A very different example of dealing with trauma is the case of a 42-year-old man named Eric, who became ill from a rapidly growing, cancerous tumor. Because of his poor prognosis, he became depressed and felt suicidal; he wanted to take his own life before the tumor did. He didn't want his life to be controlled by events. He had been a dynamic, successful executive and was not used to being passive and helpless.

However, he had a very good response to both an operation and chemotherapy, and once he saw that he had a chance at survival, his depression lifted a bit and he went into his coping mode, which included agitation and a certain amount of grandiosity. He fantasized about how he was going to get cured and how, after he was cured, he was going to dedicate his life to curing the whole world of malignancies and raising funds for cancer research and services. Post-surgery and post-chemotherapy he continued to be agitated and grandiose, and also got very aggressive with his wife and children. They were concerned that some of this was a result of the chemotherapy or that he might have had some central nervous system damage from the chemotherapy, despite the fact that, according to tests, the tumor had not gotten into the central nervous system. He was sent to a psychiatrist, who just wanted to put him on medication and monitor him once a month.

Eric came to see us because he and his wife were concerned about the effect all of this was having on their three children and he was receiving very little treatment in the vein described above. Meanwhile, his wife had become depressed and overwhelmed. Not only was she not very nurturing and engaging with him, but she, herself, required considerable help, and the children were very agitated and frightened. They were acting out at school, getting into trouble, and not doing their homework. Therefore, the first step was to settle the family down and find a nurturing, empathetic therapist who could work with the whole family to establish routines and reestablish a sense of safety and security.

We worked on the communication between Eric and his wife, so that they could hear each other and calm each other down. Eric also needed more intensive talking therapy in which he could explore his grandiose plans and the scary, overwhelming, and helpless feelings that were underneath those plans, so he started seeing the family therapist three times a week by himself. Couples therapy and family therapy helped the family to be more caring and interactive and secure with each other. This allowed Eric's wife to calm down and be more available and nurturing once again.

With this pattern of care, especially the aspect of reestablishing a sense of nurturing engagement and security in the family, Eric was able to calm down enough to really get into his feelings in therapy. Then the grandiosity, agitation, and aggressive behaviors subsided and he was able to approach the fifth step of healing—helping others—in a more realistic way. Through his company, he started a foundation to raise money for research on the type of tumor he'd had, and felt grateful for the opportunity to give something back to the community. A moderately religious person before his illness, Eric now became a little more religious. Grateful for having survived, he vowed to lead a more balanced life, and he became active in community organizations as well as becoming a more nurturing and empathetic father and more focused on family life.

Eventually Eric discontinued the medication he had been prescribed for agitation right after the illness. However, his personal therapy continued for about four years after the event. After security, engagement, and communication had been established, he was able to work with the therapist on the feelings level in a specific way, which allowed him to work through the trauma of an acute illness, as well as his issues surrounding being ill in general, after a lifetime of good health.

Points to Remember

A treatment plan for individuals who have experienced trauma in their lives should begin as soon as possible after the traumatic event (without, however, forcing the individual to discuss the event before he or she is ready) should include the following principles:

- Restore a sense of safety and security.
- Reestablish relationship and engagement with a trusted loved one.
- Encourage communication–if necessary, nonverbally at first.
- Help the person tell the story of the traumatic event in her own way.
- Involve the person in doing something active to help others.

Chapter 15

Memory Loss

Memory loss may not seem to belong in the same category as the mental health disorders we've been discussing, but in fact it is a common challenge among the elderly, and affects them and those they live with and love just as mental health disorders do. Fortunately, it can be addressed using the techniques described for other challenges. There is a similarity between the elderly experiencing memory loss, adults with traumatic brain injuries who lose (temporarily, it is to be hoped) their ability to speak or use ideas, children with developmental challenges, and young children who are not yet speaking or using ideas to any great degree.

What these groups have in common is a reliance on pre-verbal—or pre-symbolic—memory and experience. The recognition of experience that occurs outside the realm of ideas (which can be remembered in a profound way through one's emotions) has important implications for how we can create healing relationships for the elderly with memory loss, as well as for other groups of people.

Robert and Harold

Let's look at the case of a 95-year-old gentleman we'll call Robert, who was diagnosed with Alzheimer's disease and has a lot of memory loss. Robert is frequently confused about where he is and who is taking care of him, but he always has a big smile on his face and always seems happy. In addition to his wife, Robert has a companion and helper for six to seven hours a day—a man in his late 60s named Harold. Harold is in quite good health and helps with some of the physical aspects of Robert's care—the eating, grooming, and so forth. Harold, too, always seems in good spirits; he's always joking, always positive, always very warm and nurturing, and he clearly has a good relationship with Robert.

Whenever he sees Harold, Robert gets a big smile on his face and his eyes light up. Yet, if you ask him who Harold is, he can't tell you. He can talk about wanting to eat or his vital needs, but he wouldn't be able to tell you Harold's name. However, when Harold was ill for a couple of days and didn't spend time with Robert, Robert became very depressed and forlorn, almost like a baby whose mother goes away for a couple of days. He was also less functional than usual. He walked less, he expressed fewer words to get his basic needs met, he seemed more preoccupied; his wife was quite concerned. When Harold came back, Robert's smile returned and it was a smile of recognition.

Many nurturing, supportive wives of men with Alzheimer's have said that, although their husbands don't know anyone else in the family anymore, "He always recognizes me, gives me a big smile whenever I come into the room, and seems reassured when I'm there." Some colleagues think this is simply a fantasy on the wife's part, but we disagree strongly. We think there is an emotional recognition, just as Robert has for Harold and for his wife, of nurturing caregivers, even with the memory loss at the level of names.

Robert's family has known that he has had Alzheimer's for at least 10 years. He and his wife live in a retirement village with few supports. Robert recently was found wandering aimlessly around the grounds, not fully clothed. This kind of thing had happened to him occasionally before, such as when visiting relatives. He was evaluated by a psychiatrist and consultants to the retirement village, and was given a "diagnosis of Alzheimer's." The community said that they weren't equipped to handle Alzheimer's cases, and that the family should consider whether another place would be better. They didn't insist that Robert leave, but just indicated that this community wasn't the ideal place for him now that he's been diagnosed with Alzheimer's. But again, Robert had in fact had Alzheimer's for ten years, he was familiar with his physical surroundings, he liked his apartment and so did his wife, and he was doing well with Harold.

Nonetheless, the family was ready to move him to another city to be close to extended family. Instead of being down south where it was warm, he was going to move up to one of the major cities in the northeast with his son, daughter-in-law, and the daughter-in-law's extended family. The idea was that he would either go into a nursing home or have in-home nursing care, which would be much better for his condition. The family was convinced that he would be much happier in this situation, but Robert's wife wasn't sure, because this plan meant that Robert would lose Harold because Harold wasn't prepared to move as well.

Fortunately, Robert's wife had the intuition and the assertiveness to veto the plan and say that Harold was too important to Robert for them to move. However, some of Robert's children took the strict medical perspective and felt that he had to be in an Alzheimer's specialty care facility. So the family was at a crossroads, and one of the children asked for our opinion. We told him that we agreed with the wife, that Harold was the key person in considering what was best for Robert. If they were separated, Robert probably wouldn't survive emotionally and therefore his physical health would deteriorate as well. His children felt that, at 95, Robert didn't have long to live anyhow, but we believed that such a profound loss would speed up the process considerably.

This recommendation was not based simply on theory. We have seen similar cases on each side of the ledger, situations in which a person with Alzheimer's or severe memory loss from other causes was separated from a very close, nurturing relationship with a caretaker and moved to a different location. In half of the cases the individuals did very well with the transition—staying fairly healthy until some natural event took their lives—and in the other half of the cases, a change of caretakers and physical location led to marked deterioration.

In one typical example of the latter situation, a woman with mild-to-moderate Alzheimer's who had never married or had children was being looked after by a much younger friend, as well as an in-home nurse. As soon as she was moved to a nursing home facility to take care of her greater medical needs, she started getting pneumonia and other illnesses, her memory deteriorated very rapidly, and within a year she had passed away. We were concerned that this would happen to Robert, as he did indeed recognize and remember his wife and Harold enough to feel their loss. He knew them in a far deeper way than just being able to express their names in words. He had an emotional feeling about them.

The Nature of Preverbal Experience and Interaction

This gets us to the nature of preverbal experience and how we organize it. What is Robert actually experiencing when he sees Harold and lights up? Going back to our stages of development, we see that the first four stages have to do with preverbal experience: the basic sense of security that comes from being calm and focused, the feeling of engagement with a caring, nurturing primary caregiver, the back-and-forth emotional signaling through which an infant develops a sense of an individual self because he is getting a response to his signals, and then the stage of shared problem-solving, of back-and-forth preverbal communication that gives the child a sense of being able to master his environment, of operating as a self within larger patterns of interaction.

All people with very good marriages or friendships have a relationship that's solid in these first four levels: they are secure with one another; they are engaged and feel a sense of intimacy; they read and respond to each other's emotional signals; and they problem-solve and negotiate together, which gives each of them a larger sense of who they are as a person. They know when to expect annoyance, support, or pride and admiration, all within a larger pattern of social interaction. All of these levels occur in typically developing infants and toddlers before ideas and verbal language become established.

Memory loss occurs from the top down, as it were. It starts off with the loss of ideas in higher-level abstract and logical thinking and the memory for ideas. But for most people with Alzheimer's as well as other forms of memory loss, including that resulting from traumatic brain injuries, the pre-ideational workings of the brain and the mind still organize emotional experience.

The brain is organized hierarchically to some degree, although there is lots of communication between all parts of the brain. We can think of the mind as organized according to our six levels. The lower parts of the brain have to do with basic survival and functioning. Then, there are the emotional parts of the brain, which organize emotional experience and reactions, from more primitive fight-or-flight reactions to elaborate patterns of intimacy. Then there are the higher cortical functions of planning and sequencing, and the prefrontal cortex functions of auditory and verbal language in the left side of the brain, and visual-spatial and symbolic experiences in the right side of the brain.

What we are suggesting is that the first four levels of the mind are intact for Robert, so he recognizes Harold; he experiences Harold in terms of the security of the first level, the intimacy of the second level, the emotional signaling of the third level, and the shared problem-solving of the fourth level. In terms of Robert's brain functioning, these levels include the basic lower parts of the brain having to do with regulation and survival, the middle parts having to do with emotions and the organization of emotions, and components of the cortical parts having to do with sequencing and problem-solving, but not the higher symbolic areas having to do with memory. (In the later stages of Alzheimer's, sometimes all the parts of the brain deteriorate, including the parts that support basic functions like breathing and eating, and then we often see rapid deterioration in physical health. Fortunately, many people with Alzheimer's never get to that stage.)

Thus, Robert and many individuals like Robert are very, very attuned to their emotional worlds and have very good memories of emotional experiences, but not in words or ideas. It is similar to the way a 15-month-old or a nonverbal three- or four-year-old has an emotional experience. This kind of emotional experience is just as valid as a verbal one; in some ways it is even more intense because the person doesn't have the verbal or symbolic abilities to negotiate with the world, and can't use ideas to cover up emotions or distance himself from emotions. At the same time, it is harder to get one's needs met without language and ideas, so if Robert, for example, is dependent on Harold, he is more likely to panic and feel helpless if Harold isn't there.

This picture of preverbal emotional experience is supported by studies of children in hospitals. In the 1940s, it was observed that when children were separated from their parents to go into the hospital for a couple of weeks, and the parents couldn't stay with their children and lived too far away to visit often, the children got depressed and their emotional and physical health deteriorated to some degree. The Robertsons made films of children in hospitals showing these profound reactions, and Bowlby and Spitz, two pioneers in infant research in the 1940s, also documented children in orphanages and hospitals. They coined the term "hospitalism" for children who were well cared for and well fed physically, but didn't have a constant nurturing figure. Many of these children failed to gain weight or had "failure to thrive," meaning their physical development was stunted. Others failed to develop in terms of language or in other ways, and others developed physically but lacked the capacity for intimacy, so they became somewhat anti-social, as well as very promiscuous. They were coping with their environment, but without that intimacy of the nurturing relationship.

These phenomena are also seen in infants and young children in families where there has been a lot of emotional deprivation. And we see this in some children from orphanages where there isn't a constant nurturing figure; they have many features similar to children with autistic spectrum disorders. So, there is a lot of evidence that emotional experience is very important preverbally, pre-ideationally, and it's no less important for the elderly, and probably no less important for those with traumatic brain injuries.

Healing Relationships for Individuals with Memory Loss

What implication do these studies have for healing relationships and environments for the elderly and for people with injury-induced memory loss? In the case of Robert, the fact that his very intelligent children were ready to move their father from his relationship with Harold, and they were being supported by a psychiatrist in this, shows that there is not yet full understanding of the importance of preverbal emotional experiences. The justification that "he doesn't know what is going on anyhow," is hardly the case.

Robert knows what is going on; he just can't experience it at the level of ideas or logical thinking. Emotionally, however, he knows it in some ways better than a very verbal person would, as does a 15-month old toddler whose mother goes away. Many parents have had the experience of coming home after a week's business trip and getting the cold shoulder from their toddler for a while. The toddler's negative behavior is not by chance; it's an expression of the child's anger and hurt at being deserted.

In the context of this understanding of emotion and verbal memory, what is the best way to help people with memory loss? First, we should operate from the principle that, the more memory loss an individual has, the more important it is for him to have a primary relationship with a caregiver who is very nurturing and supportive, who brings a gleam to the person's eye, whether in a nursing home or at the person's home. And that caregiver should be constant. So, nursing homes should keep staff assigned to the same individuals, rather than moving them from floor to floor. This constant relationship should be the top priority, because it determines the person's physical health as well as emotional and intellectual health. Therefore, if we are putting someone in an Alzheimer facility to get better care, it will have the opposite effect if we're separating a "Robert" from a "Harold." In such a case, the person would be much better off staying in whatever situation can maintain the relationship; we can bring in extra caregivers if necessary.

With this relationship as a baseline, the next step is to support the areas of mental development that are still functioning well, so that they don't deteriorate. In Robert's case and in most cases, this means supporting the preverbal levels of development. Thus, we first want to support regulation and security through lots of soothing, relaxing, sensory experiences. Just as we do for infants, every elderly person with memory loss or adult with traumatic brain injury should have lots of tactile input, including massage, as well as soothing verbal chitchat and soothing visual experiences. Some prefer firm pressure, others lighter touch, but skillful massage is important to any program. We also want to include enjoyable sensory experiences relating to textures, tastes, scents, and sights, as well as touch.

The key here—as with our programs for other mental health challenges—is to adapt the program to the individual. If the person is hyperalert or vigilant, we should make the environment and the interactions very soothing and quiet. If the person is withdrawn and self-absorbed, we want to create an energetic, interesting environment. We want to do whatever is necessary to help the person attend to the world in a calm, regulated fashion. Then we want to support engagement through the primary nurturing relationship—the caregiver who spends hours a day with the person, whom the person enjoys being with. Engagement can take place around the most basic of activities, holding the person's hand, helping him eat and bathe, giving a massage, as well as an adult version of Floortime to keep back-and-forth interaction going.

This gets us to the third level of development: exchanging emotional signals, through gestures as well as words, and doing a lot of problem-solving together. It's important to get the person physically active—moving around, finding things, participating in his own care—with you as an active partner. Rather than just doing things for the person, get him involved by asking, for example, "Do you want juice? Where is the fridge? Which glass should we use?" Go to the fridge together and look for things. Play dumb, and encourage the person to remember where something is, for example. If she can't, give her two choices, saying, "Do you think it's here or there?" You'll be exchanging some words if the person is verbal, as well as pointing and gesturing and problem-solving together. It is a very respectful attitude. Challenge the person to be assertive and take initiative as much as possible.

As much as possible, we want to preserve any verbal ability that is there. Use it to empower the person to make choices that require thought. What would he like to eat? Which TV show would he like to watch? Which friend would he like to see? Would he like to go for a walk or a ride in the car? Don't use memorized scripts; instead, play to opinions and choices and have long conversations. If the person is verbal, as many individuals with memory loss are, but only in terms of the present moment (he can't remember what he asked for a few minutes ago, for example), then work in the here-and-now with opinions and choices, with present likes and dislikes, and the reasons for those choices. Of course, all this should be done in a very soothing, nurturing way, not pressuring the person to deliver but encouraging him to be involved. We return to essayist and author Anne Lamott's writing about her mother, "I took her everywhere, included her every chance I could, and tended to her daily when she got sick with Alzheimer's. She floated away on the riptide of dementia, ultimately a speck on the horizon, waving for as long as she could to her deeply confused children onshore." (p. 227) Lamott did all she could to maintain her mother's quality of life as her mental health declined.

Finally, as much as possible we want to have physical consistency as well as emotional consistency. Don't change the physical environment. If the person is living in a home that is familiar, it's better (and less expensive) to have nursing care in the home, rather than moving the person to a facility. You can have a helper in the home and a nurse come in periodically for medication checks or health checks. If you must use a nursing home, make sure it is a very nurturing place where the person can keep a feeling of familiarity; his furniture should go with him and the room should be set up in a familiar way. As much as is possible, keep the physical setting consistent.

These techniques can help the elderly with memory loss stay healthier longer, and can also be helpful for the recovery of traumatic brain injuries, particularly gradually exposing the person to more and more sensory and motor and language experience in the context of these first four levels of development. Whether the person can talk about it or not, emotional experience exists, and healing relationships and environments tune in to these first four levels of development and respect them. Let's hope that Robert's family has the wisdom not to take him from the person who has been keeping a big smile on Robert's face for many years.

Points to Remember

We can help elderly people with memory loss–whether from Alzheimer's or traumatic brain injury–to maintain their faculties as much as possible (and perhaps to recover, in the case of brain injuries) by using many of the principles we've established for the mental health disorders described in this book, as well as the following:

- Because emotional memory lasts much longer than verbal memory, long-term, positive relationships with close caregivers should be maintained as long as possible, rather than separating the person from someone who brings them joy.
- Support the preverbal levels of development through soothing sensory experiences, engagement, and back-and-forth, problem-solving interactions tailored to the person's profile.
- Maintain a consistent physical environment as much as possible.

Chapter 16

Asperger's Syndrome

Like memory loss, Asperger's Syndrome is not generally considered to be a mental illness *per se,* but many of the principles discussed in this book also apply to individuals with Asperger's Syndrome. Asperger's Syndrome is being diagnosed with increasing frequency in children, adolescents, and young adults who have difficulty or awkwardness with social relationships or reading social signals, who tend to be rigid or inflexible in their thinking, who may use language logically but lack an understanding of subtlety and nuance, who have trouble making inferences or being creative in their use of ideas, and/or who tend to get overwhelmed.

From a technical point of view, the diagnosis of Asperger's Syndrome should only be used for individuals who meet the criteria for an autistic spectrum disorder but who have more advanced language capacities. Often, however, the criteria for autism are not applied rigorously, and individuals who have great warmth and intimacy with one or two people (and who therefore cannot be considered autistic)—who may be very close to a parent, for example, but have more trouble reading social signals with peers or when they get overwhelmed—still receive such a diagnosis. Individuals with extreme anxiety or obsessive patterns may also receive a diagnosis of Asperger's Syndrome if their anxiety or obsessiveness interferes with their social interactions.

The important point to make is that there may be many different pathways to and combinations of symptoms that constitute what is today labeled as Asperger's Syndrome. For example, in terms of the various developmental pathways, there are people who are very reactive to sensation and who have problems planning their actions and with understanding how their bodies operate in space. Such individuals easily get overwhelmed in many situations. During the critical juncture from about 7 to 20 months of life, when nonverbal gestures and emotional expressions are being mastered (such as smiles, smirks, head nods, vocal tone, and so forth), individuals with the processing profile described above may miss out on full mastery of this whole nonverbal communication system. They are therefore less able to read complex and subtle social signals, which then throws them off the pathway to more advanced social relationships as they get older.

If they have very good memory skills they may master the logical use of language, but not the subtle skill of applying language to complex social situations. The subtleties of language such as irony or innuendo often have to do with tone of voice; just the slightest bit of change in tone, for example, is the difference between a friendly joke and making fun of someone. The tone, combined with a twinkle in the eye or a hostile look, may determine whether the person speaking is friendly or dangerous. The ability to make these kinds of judgments is not mastered, leading to the social awkwardness observed in people diagnosed with Asperger's Syndrome.

There can be other developmental reasons, besides an over-reactivity to sensation, that this stage of mastering nonverbal signals is not fully mastered and someone may be diagnosed with Asperger's Syndrome. Some children are both over-reactive to sensation and crave sensation; they have a mixed processing pattern. They may also have weaker visual-spatial capacities and visual-spatial problem solving abilities, although they have good visual memory. This means that they can't figure out how other people's bodies relate to their bodies in space, or how to throw or catch a ball, so they may have coordination and motor problems. They may have very good memories for words, and can memorize whole songs and whole passages from books, but then have trouble knowing the subtle ways to use what they've memorized. Therefore, it's incorrect to say they have advanced or even healthy language development, because really only the memory part of language is working well for them, not the pragmatic use of language, the more subtle use of language, or the use of language for abstract problem solving.

Similarly, their reading comprehension may seem good in the early years when they're required to remember facts from a passage, but later, when they have to make inferences from a passage or discuss issues such as character development, they may have a much harder time. The same thing applies to history; facts may be easy to memorize, while interpretations—understanding what motivated people in different historical eras to do what they did—are much more difficult.

On the other hand, some people have a very good and subtle reading of social cues, have good abstract reasoning, and are capable of great intimacy, but are just very over-reactive to sensation and tend to get very anxious, which gets in the way of using their subtle language skills in complex social situations. It's a mistake to label them with Asperger's Syndrome; they more accurately should be described in terms of their anxiety since they don't have the other core features of Asperger's, although they may be socially awkward because they get overwhelmed. Other individuals who are very bright and creative and capable of great intimacy—but who are very under-reactive to sensation and tend to live in their fantasy worlds and are therefore not very socially adept—may also be given the label of Asperger's Syndrome. Again, this is an incorrect diagnosis.

Now that we have clarified what does and does not constitute Asperger's Syndrome, let's address what to do about it and how to be most helpful to individuals with this pattern. These principles apply to children, adolescents, and adults. The key point is that you get what you practice, so teaching someone to memorize rules for social interactions is the wrong approach. Remember, people with Asperger's Syndrome have a natural tendency to rely on their strong memories to learn rote rules for complex social situations that require instead a subtle reading of cues, the ability to make inferences, and the use of abstract and reflective thinking capacities. Rather than working to strengthen the developmental pathways toward mastery of nonverbal and gestural interaction, they feel more comfortable with rules for greeting people, saying goodbye, and so forth. But such an approach really digs the hole deeper because there are millions, if not billions, of rules that could apply to complex social situations. Memorizing all the rules is an impossible task.

The real goal is to teach people to be what we consider intuitive in social situations, that is, to have a very rapid pre-conscious process of reading signals and responding. So the best approach is to help individuals back on to the healthy developmental pathway that they missed initially. This means giving them lots of practice with social interactions in which they can learn to read facial expressions and nuances, not giving them pictures of faces to label according to memorized rules about what constitutes a "happy" face, a "sad" face, a "mad" face, and so forth. They need to spend hours and hours interacting with one person, with several people, with many people, to begin to get a feel for social cues and nuances. It's analogous to learning a foreign language in a full immersion program where you go to the country and live among the people who speak the language, rather than learning from a textbook or in a class that meets for only a few hours a week. It's a more natural way of learning the language.

The challenge is to facilitate this type of learning without triggering the person's anxiety and overwhelming him. The way to do this is to work within the framework of the six developmental levels, so the first step is to create a situation in which the person feels calm, regulated, and secure. If he is over-reactive to sensation, he's not going to feel calm in a busy, noisy, crowded setting; it has to be a quiet setting. Then, he needs to feel engaged and warm and intimate. He may not be able to verbalize these feelings, but nonetheless he can experience them within certain relationships, perhaps with a parent, a sibling, or a good friend who's warm and empathetic. Sometimes it may need to be a therapeutic relationship with a therapist; the important thing is that it is someone who is there for him in a supportive way, with whom he can feel close and engaged.

Then, as we interact with him in a quiet setting, we'll want to be animated, but not overwhelming. We should be expressive and emotive so that our nonverbal signals—facial expressions, hand gestures, shoulder shrugs, smiles, winks, and so forth—are fairly clear, along with our words. We should also engage the person in creative activities and logical conversations. For an adult, the creative activities might be drawing or sculpting or writing creative stories together. For a teenager, they might be making little movies, writing stories, or engaging in a hobby together in a creative way. For example, if the teenager likes to look at maps and memorize geography facts, we want to go for the opinions, saying, "Well, which country would you rather live in, and why?" Use the facts as a jumping-off point for thinking and creative problem-solving.

For a child, pretend play is the best creative activity as we can both be characters in the child's drama. The idea is to start with what interests the child, even if it's just lining up toy cars in a row, and then gradually expand that drama. We might ask, "Well, which cars are better and faster?" Maybe the cars start talking to each other, or you have a car race. The first step is simply to get more emotion and expression into the interaction without trying to label the feelings; let the feelings evolve naturally through the interaction. Watch the child's face to see if she becomes a little more animated, a little more expressive, and try to entice that along.

Whether you are working with a child, adolescent, or adult, the goal is to gradually increase the person's flexibility around social interaction, without worrying about the words yet, by increasing the range of emotion. Gradually, we want to help expand the person's comfort with the emotions that tend to be more problematic, such as competition or conflict and aggression. We might start this by saying something like, "Gee, I don't want to do that today," when it comes time to do a regular activity that the person likes, for example. Of course, this is said gently, from a place of warmth and intimacy, allowing the person to address the conflict around what to do without withdrawing or getting defensive.

Usually aggression and assertiveness are very frightening, so once the person can handle a little bit of conflict, then she is probably ready to start talking about feelings. Now, it could take many months or even years for the person to get to the stage of being expressive around a wide range of emotions. But once she has this increased flexibility with nonverbal expression, then we can help her label and talk about her own feelings and those of others. One way to approach this is through the "Thinking About Tomorrow" game, described in earlier chapters. This allows the person to explore her emotions and options in a secure context.

Then, once the person can express the full range of feelings, we want to gradually increase the complexity of the social situations in which he feels comfortable—from just one person to a couple people to a small group—and the complexity of the sensory environment—from quiet and calm to one that's a bit noisier or busier. Increasing the person's tolerance is a very, very gradual process. The key thing is to move slowly and always provide support for the basics: security, regulation, intimate engagement and a lot of interaction with a trusted, reliable person.

As the person becomes more verbal and more reflective, we can move into a process that's more like regular psychotherapy: helping him explore his feelings and the feelings of others, and talk about what's easy and what's hard for him. We should anticipate a long-term relationship as a therapist, parent, teacher, or anyone else in a helping relationship with someone with Asperger's Syndrome, because he'll always need us in his corner to provide a secure base.

While we are helping the person progress through the developmental levels, we also want to strengthen some of the weaker processing areas. So, if someone's weak area is body coordination or body awareness, we want to have a program that includes strengthening motor skills through fun activities several times a day—perhaps sports, dancing, or yoga. If the person is weak in visual-spatial thinking, we want to help him improve his ability to see the world from different angles and perspectives. We can strengthen verbal abstract reasoning through natural conversations about history and literature and culture, always using the personal approach that projects the individual into the situation by asking, "Well, how would you feel in that situation? How would you feel if you lived in that culture, if you lived in that historical time?"

So, working with someone with Asperger's Syndrome is a very gradual process, as we fill in the developmental steps that were missed. This is what we want the environment or the family or the therapy team to provide. Sometimes anxiety medications may be helpful for certain individuals, to reduce their response to sensory overload so they're not in panic mode and can relax and read social signals a little better. Finally, in terms of education or employment, it's important to help people with this challenge explore interests and work situations that allow them some control over their environment—where they won't be overloaded or overwhelmed, where they can control how much social interaction they have, and yet where there are opportunities for warm, nurturing relationships.

Points to Remember

When Asperger's is an appropriate diagnosis, it is best to work with the person in a developmental framework using the following as general principles. Remember that "you get what you practice."

- Take into account the person's unique processing sensitivities, strengthen the early stages of development through lots of practice with social interactions that are regulating and engaging.

- Engage the person in many creative and logical interactions and activities.
- Work with the person to increase emotional flexibility in social interactions.
- Strengthen the person's processing abilities.
- Incorporate life choices, such as careers, that are best suited to the person's profile.

Conclusion

In this book, we have attempted to take what might be called a common-sense or layman's approach to the most common mental health disorders. Looking through a developmental lens, we've identified the pathway, or developmental sequence, associated with each of the disorders. The pathways invariably involve some biologically based differences, but these are not always expressed directly in the disorder; rather, they express themselves through differences in the sensory and motor systems and ways of processing affect. Then, various developmental experiences may contribute to the disorder. They may intensify these biological patterns or ameliorate them, as in the example of bipolar disorders where the steps of counter-balancing and mood regulation can help, whereas joining the child in his mood swings intensifies the problem. Finally, with most of the disorders, we want to help the person move up the developmental ladder in terms of thinking abilities: first becoming more elaborative and imaginative so he can play out his feelings, then learning to connect ideas together so he can verbalize his feelings and eventually reflect on his feelings, moving from causal thinking to comparative thinking, to gray-area thinking, and then to reflective thinking.

Through our understanding of the developmental pathways for the most common mental health disorders—the biological and experiential developmental sequences involved—we can develop a comprehensive treatment approach that involves professionals, family members, and key relationships in the individual's life. Most importantly, the person with the disorder can learn to identify the contributing components more fully, and so becomes able to help himself more effectively. This self-awareness also means that the person's relationships with family members, significant others, and therapists are more helpful. This provides the basis for a comprehensive partnership between the individual, the family, those in important relationships with the individual, and professionals.

Thus, the aim of this book is to serve as a comprehensive guide for anyone affected by mental health disorders—those individuals with the disorders, and the people in their lives. My colleagues and we believe that bringing a developmental lens to these disorders provides an additional knowledge base that continues to expand. While we continue to discover more about the developmental sequence and pathways to disorders, it's important to apply what we already know, and to encourage others to join us in this effort. In this way, we can help to mend the tattered inner security blankets so that people have sufficient warmth and comfort to live full and happy lives.

References

Bowlby, J. (1951). *Maternal care and mental health.* WHO Monograph Series, no. 51. Geneva: World Health Organization.

Furth, H. and Wachs, H. (1975). *Thinking Goes to School: Piaget's Theory in Practice.* Oxford University Press.

Greenspan, S. I. (1992) *Infancy and Early Childhood: The Practice of Clinical Assessment and Intervention with Emotional and Developmental Challenges.* Madison, CT: International Universities Press.

Greenspan, S.I. (2001). *The Four-Thirds Solution: Solving the Child-Care Crisis in America Today.* Cambridge, MA: Perseus Publishing.

Greenspan, S.I. (2002). *The Secure Child: Helping Our Children Feel Safe and Confident in an Insecure World.* Cambridge, MA: Perseus Publishing.

Greenspan, S. I., Glovinsky, C., and Glovinsky, I. (2007). *Children and Babies with Mood Swings: New Insights for Parents and Professionals.* Bethesda, MD: Interdisciplinary Council on Developmental and Learning Disorders.

Greenspan, S.I. and Salmon, J. (1993). *Playground Politics: The Emotional Development of Your School-Aged Child.* Reading, MA: Addison Wesley Publishers.

Greenspan, S.I. and Salmon, J. (1995). *The Challenging Child: Understanding, Raising, and Enjoying the Five "Difficult" Types of Children.* Reading, MA: Addison Wesley Publishers.

Greenspan, S. I. and Shanker, S. G. (2004). *The First Idea: How Symbols, Language and Intelligence Evolved in Early Primates and Humans.* Reading, MA: Perseus Books.

Greenspan, S. I. and Wieder, S. (1998). *The Child with Special Needs: Intellectual and Emotional Growth.* Reading, MA: Addison Wesley Longman

Greenspan, S. I. and Wieder, S. (2005). *Infant and Early Childhood Mental Health: A Comprehensive Developmental Approach to Assessment and Intervention.* Arlington, VA: American Psychiatric Publishing, Inc.

Greenspan, S.I., Weider, S., Lieberman, A., Nover, R., Lourie, R., and Robinson, M. (1987). Infants in Multirisk Families: Case Studies in Preventive Intervention. *Clinical Infant Reports,* No. 3. New York: International Universities Press.

Lamott, A. (2007). *Grace (eventually).* NY: Riverhead Books.

McKibben, B. (2007) *Deep economy*. NY: Henry Holt and Company.

Spitz, R. A. (1945). Hospitalism: An inquiry into the genesis of psychiatric conditions in early childhood. *The Psychoanalytic Study of the Child* 1:53–74.